# *embroidered* ANIMAL PORTRAITS

## A GUIDE TO THREAD PAINTING FUR, FEATHERS, SPINES & SCALES

*Michelle Staub* OF STITCHING SABBATICAL

**stash**BOOKS®

*an imprint of C&T Publishing*

PUBLISHER: Amy Barrett-Daffin

CREATIVE DIRECTOR: Gailen Runge

SENIOR EDITOR: Roxane Cerda

EDITOR: Madison Moore

TECHNICAL EDITOR: Jessica Schunke

COVER/BOOK DESIGNER: April Mostek

PRODUCTION COORDINATOR: Tim Manibusan

ILLUSTRATOR: Kirstie Pettersen, Michelle Staub

PHOTOGRAPHY COORDINATOR: Rachel Ackley

FRONT COVER PHOTOGRAPHY by Michelle Staub

PHOTOGRAPHY by Michelle Staub, unless otherwise noted

Published by Stash Books, an imprint of C&T Publishing, Inc., P.O. Box 1456, Lafayette, CA 94549

Library of Congress Cataloging-in-Publication Data

Names: Staub, Michelle, 1992- author.

Title: Embroidered animal portraits : a guide to thread painting fur, feathers, spines & scales / Michelle Staub.

Description: Lafayette, CA : StashBooks, an imprint of C&T Publishing, [2024] | Summary: "Join embroidery artist Michelle Staub for another master class in thread painting, this time focusing on twelve new animals! Inside covers everything readers need to get started in thread painting like basic stitches, various turning photos into embroidery designs, full lessons, and more, in order to create stunning embroideredmasterpieces"-- Provided by publisher.

Identifiers: LCCN 2024009529 | ISBN 9781644034552 (trade paperback) | ISBN 9781644034569 (ebook)

Subjects: LCSH: Embroidery--Patterns. | Decoration and ornament--Animal forms. | BISAC: CRAFTS & HOBBIES / Needlework / Embroidery | CRAFTS & HOBBIES / Fiber Arts & Textiles

Classification: LCC TT773 .S723 2024 | DDC 746.44/041--dc23/eng/20240329

LC record available at https://lccn.loc.gov/2024009529

Printed in China

10 9 8 7 6 5 4 3 2 1

# Dedication

*This book is dedicated to my son, Abel. I hope you grow up with love, care, and tenderness for all animals from furry to feathery and everything in between.*

## ACKNOWLEDGMENTS

This book was only possible to create because of the people who so generously allowed me to use their photos as references. A big thank you to Ashley Danh, Adam Wachtel, Susan Ussler, Brenda Snyman, Sandy Entrena Ramos, Taylor Wong (@ChonkyTheHedgehog), Cintia Szuhai, Allison Funneman, Mary Hilton, Ellie's Exotics, Kendall Thornhill, Dan Trout, and Emily Streich.

This endeavor would not have been possible without my husband encouraging me throughout the process and helping me put all of my disorganized thoughts into coherent sentences. Thank you to my family who supported me and provided me with endless hours of babysitting as I spent late nights stitching and writing this book.

Finally, a thank you to C&T Publishing for encouraging me to write a second book and for going on this journey with me.

# CONTENTS

Introduction ............................................................. 6

How to Use This Book ........................................ 7

Materials and Tools .............................................. 8

Building a Design ................................................. 12

   CHOOSING A REFERENCE PHOTO ..................... 13

   CREATING A COMPOSITION .............................. 17

   CREATING A PATTERN ...................................... 19

   TRANSFERRING A PATTERN ............................... 22

Thread Painting Techniques ............................ 24

   GETTING STARTED ............................................ 25

   THREAD PAINTING AND STITCHING TEXTURES .. 26

   CREATING TEXTURE .......................................... 30

   CHOOSING COLORS .......................................... 37

Portrait Accents .................................................... 38

Finishing the Hoop .............................................. 44

## Fur, Feathers, Spines, and Scales: THREAD PAINTED PORTRAITS

Fur, Feathers, Spines, and Scales: THREAD PAINTED PORTRAITS ........................ 46

RABBIT
*Hops*
48

HAMSTER
*Madame Fluffypants*
54

GUINEA PIG
*Miru*
62

RAT
*Boonie*
68

FERRET
*Bob*
74

HEDGEHOG
*Chonky*
82

HORSE
*Fatima*
90

CHICKEN
*Natasha*
98

BUDGIE
*Milo*
106

SNAKE
*Viggo*
114

BETTA FISH
*Dalí*
120

BEARDED DRAGON
*Sushi*
130

Patterns ........................ 140

Resources ........................ 143

About the Author ........................ 144

# INTRODUCTION

I have spent the majority of my embroidery career creating stitched portraits of cats and dogs. Celebrating the bond people have with their pets is so near and dear to my heart. After years of learning how to capture their personalities with needle and thread, I wrote a book, *Pet Portrait Embroidery*, that has taught thousands of people around the world how to create their own cat and dog portraits. Through embroidery, we have celebrated the connections we share with our furry friends and created keepsakes that highlight their importance in our lives.

Now I am exploring the diverse world of pet portraits that go beyond cats and dogs. Our spiny and scaly friends are just as important and special as the typical furry friend!

Lizards, snakes, hedgehogs, birds, fish, and all other kinds of pets hold their own places in our hearts and deserve to be celebrated as much as any other. What better way to show your love for your feathered, scaly, furry, or spiny companion than through a detailed portrait you embroidered yourself?

Any embroidery, whether it depicts fur, feathers, spines, or scales, is manageable if you take your time and go slowly. This book covers a wide range of pets, but with practice, you can apply what you learn from the patterns to all sorts of subjects!

There are hundreds of bird species you can stitch with what you learn about feathers. You can make other small mammals such as chinchillas, gerbils, sugar gliders, and even squirrels with what you learn about stitching fur. Take what you learn from stitching scales and embroider other lizards, snakes, and fish! The possibilities are endless.

When you're ready, grab a needle, some thread, a hoop, and fabric. Together we'll create art that celebrates and commemorates the bond we share with all of our pets, large and small.

# HOW TO USE THIS BOOK

There are many mediums in which to create pet and animal portraits, but embroidery is by far my favorite. The tactility of the thread brings another dimension of realness to the portrait—one that can be felt. Start by reviewing the technique chapters to get the hang of thread painting (using a variety of stitch lengths and directions to create the different spiny, furry, feathery, and scaly textures) and working from a reference photo to create a realistic portrait.

This book gives you the tools to create a wide variety of animal portraits. Follow along with the provided patterns and learn how to capture the nuances of fur, feathers, spines, and scales in an animal's face. Stitch the patterns as they are, or customize them to make them look like an animal you know.

Each pattern in this book comes equipped with a color palette, a stitch direction guide, and a comprehensive series of step-by-step photos. There are a lot of colors needed for each portrait, and sometimes you may only use one or two stitches of a color. As you buy the colors needed for these projects, however, you'll build a collection of thread to use for future portraits.

The difficulty level of the patterns ranges from beginner to intermediate. The patterns in this book are very meticulous and often use a lot of small stitches. Take your time to work through the pattern,

stopping as needed. You may find it necessary to use a magnifying lens to avoid straining your eyes.

Within each of the book's categories, the portraits become progressively more complex. If you are a beginning embroiderer, working through the projects in order will give you the practice needed to complete the most intricate ones. With more experience, you may choose to attempt the more complex pieces first. Either way, I hope this book will help you on your embroidery journey!

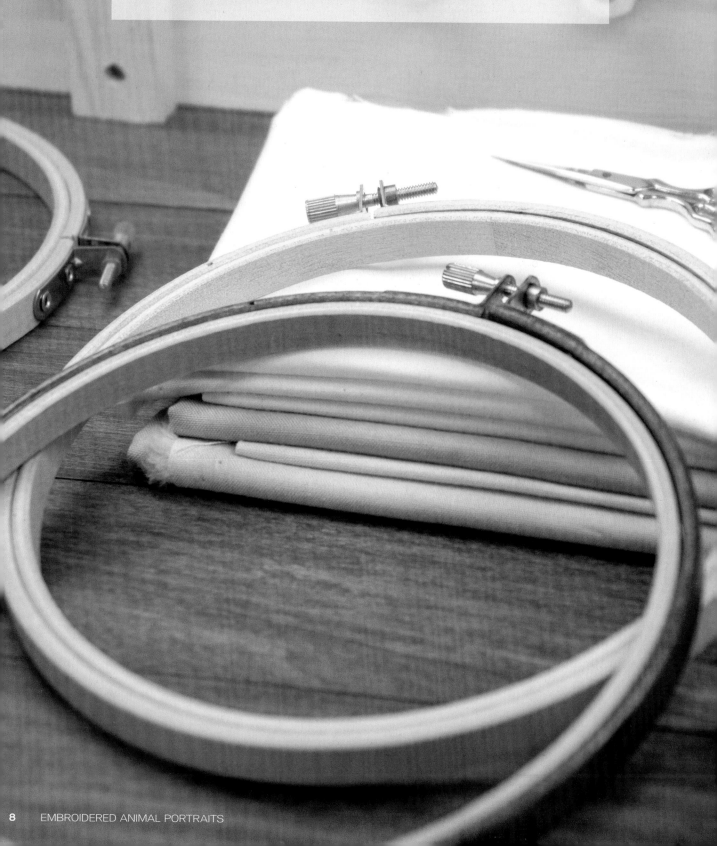

# MATERIALS AND TOOLS

## FABRIC

It's best to choose a fabric that is tightly woven, not too thin, and not stretchy. A medium-weight fabric works well since you'll be making a large number of stitches, but you may choose a heavier weight if that is your preference. If the fabric you choose is thin, or if you prefer additional stability and opacity, use two pieces of fabric layered together in the hoop. Linen, cotton, and calico are common embroidery fabrics. I stitch all of the portraits pictured in this book on a double layer of Kona Cotton from Robert Kaufman Fabrics.

## HOOPS

There are many different sizes and styles of embroidery hoops. The most common ones are made from wood or plastic and have a metal screw closure at the top to tighten the hoop. Hoop sizes can range from smaller than 3″ to larger than 14″ (8–35.6cm). I recommend cutting the fabric a minimum of 2″ (5cm) larger than the hoop diameter when preparing it for the hoop. The patterns in this book are designed for a 6″ (15cm) hoop, so start with a square of fabric at least 8″ × 8″ (20 × 20cm).

The embroidery hoop consists of two parts: the outer hoop and the inner hoop. The fabric goes between the two and the screw tightens the outer hoop to keep the fabric taut. It's normal to have to readjust the tightness of the fabric as you work, but if the hoop can't keep the fabric taut at all, try using two layers of fabric or wrapping the inner hoop with bias tape. This will give the hoop something to grip.

## NEEDLES

There are so many different brands, styles, and sizes of needles that it's easy to get overwhelmed! The one thing to remember is that the size of the needle should correspond to the number of strands of embroidery thread you're stitching with. The more strands you're working with, the larger the embroidery needle should be. I recommend starting with a multipack containing a variety of needle sizes. Needle sizes are labeled with numbers. Though it may depend on type and brand, usually larger numbers mean smaller and thinner needles; smaller numbers mean larger and thicker needles. I use a Bohin No. 10 embroidery needle for all of my single-stranded work. If I'm using two or more strands of thread, I like the John James No. 7. Sharps, chenille, crewel, or milliners—all different styles of needles—can be used for embroidery. The differences between these types of needles are in their characteristics beyond eye size, such as their length, the shape of their eyes, and their sharpness. Choose a type you feel comfortable holding and threading. A needle threader is a helpful tool if you are having trouble threading the needles.

## THREAD

The terms *embroidery thread* and *embroidery floss* can be used interchangeably. In this book, I will be referring to it as *thread*. DMC, Anchor, and COSMO embroidery floss by LECIEN Co. are the most common brands on the market. Hand embroidery thread comes as a skein, and each skein is made up of six individual strands of thread that can be separated.

The patterns in this book primarily use DMC thread, and the numbers in the patterns correspond to DMC thread colors. Each project includes a color swatch and the DMC number so that you can choose the exact color or find a similar color based on the swatch. I've also included a link to a color conversion chart in Resources (page 143). However, if you use other brands of thread, the patterns will not look the same.

Additionally, a few patterns use cotton thread from Gütermann for fine details like whiskers.

## SCISSORS

It is best to have a large pair of sharp scissors for cutting fabric and a second pair of smaller scissors for trimming embroidery thread. The most common embroidery scissors are the classic stork scissors, but any type of small scissors with sharp, pointed blades will work just as well.

## ADDITIONAL MATERIALS

Some additional materials you might find handy include the following:

- An embroidery stand to hold the hoop so you are free to work with both hands

- Bobbins to wind thread around

- Organizer boxes for sorting and storing thread

- An overhead light with a magnifying lens so you can work on smaller detailed sections without straining your eyes

- Pinking shears to trim the fabric so the edges won't fray as you work

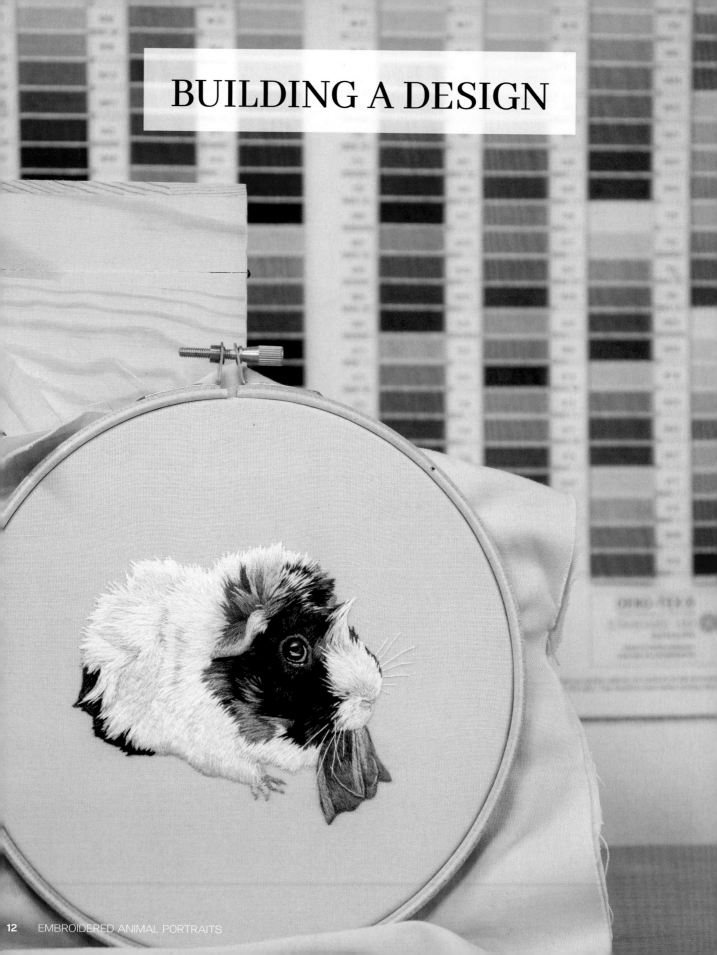

# BUILDING A DESIGN

# CHOOSING A REFERENCE PHOTO

Set yourself up for success by choosing the nicest reference photo possible. You will want to use something that both captures the essence of the animal and is well lit and clear.

## Taking Your Own Photo

Taking your own reference photo is a good option if you want to have control over the composition. You do not need any fancy equipment—most smartphones have nice cameras that will work fine. Just make sure you're in a well-lit area and have a good view of the subject at eye level. Be wary of using portrait-mode features that blur the background of the subject because sometimes it can go wrong and blur out key features of the animal.

Photo taken with portrait mode, so tail feathers and beak are accidentally blurred out. | Photo by Dan Trout

## LIGHTING

Lighting can make or break a photo. Too over- or underexposed, and you won't be able to see the details of the animal. Take the photo with a moderate amount of natural lighting. Avoid taking the photo in bright daylight, which creates harsh shadows, or indoors in areas with dim or warm lighting, which can affect the colors.

Avoid backlighting a subject. Not only will a backlit subject be poorly lit, but it can also have weird effects. For example, if you photograph a rabbit in bright sunlight, their inner ears can appear almost neon in color with many visible veins.

Photo by Gavin Allanwood / Unsplash.com

Lighting may never be optimal for some animals that live in tanks. Warm tank lighting changes how the animal looks, and it's often too dark to show all the details. Tank glass can also cast reflections over the animal. Take the animal out of its tank and into an area with better lighting if doing so is safe for both you and the animal. Angle your camera to avoid reflections if the animal must stay in the tank.

Light reflecting on the tank

Camera angled to avoid reflection on the animal

*tip* Some animals regularly shed their skin or molt their feathers. Avoid taking photos during this time as their coloring can be different or they may look a little disheveled.

## ANGLES

Take the photo at eye level to the animal. This will give you a good view of the subject. Make sure to have the entire subject in the frame if you want to embroider their whole body. The best angles for portraits are from a straight-on, profile, or three-quarter view.

## MOTION

It can be very hard to photograph small pets. It may be easier to take a video of the animal and then use a frame from the video as a reference. If your phone has a live photo option, you can use that and then select a specific frame from the photo to use. Be patient and take your time.

You might choose to give the animal a small snack to keep it still long enough to take a photo. Consider adding that snack to the portrait if it's a favorite of theirs!

Photo by Brenda Snyman

For animals like birds, it might be easiest to let them sit on your hand, your shoulder, or their favorite perch. You may leave that in their portrait or imagine them in a different scenario, like sitting on a branch or out in their natural habitat. You can pull in additional photo references to create a scene.

## CREATING A COMPOSITION

### Complement the Portrait

You want the portrait to be a cohesive piece of art.
That includes considering all aspects of the piece—the
reference photo, the pose of the animal, the position
of the embroidery in the portrait, the fabric color, and
possibly additional framing. All of these aspects can
either complement or detract from the portrait, so
plan carefully and consider each part.

## Creating a Scene

Think about the shape of the pet and how it will be framed in the composition. If your pet has a more elongated shape (horse, snake, ferret, bird, etc.), you might consider using an oval hoop for their portrait to allow more of the animal's body to be stitched.

Will you embroider the whole animal? Just its head? Perhaps your pet is centered in the middle of the portrait, or maybe part of its body extends down to the edge of the hoop so you can focus on the pet's face.

If you are stitching the full body of your pet, add some grounding so they aren't just floating alone. This can be done with a small shadow or some other decorative elements, like grass, leaves, flowers, or perhaps something that relates to their natural habitat.

The patterns in this book are meant to fit a standard 6" embroidery hoop or frame, but you may choose to display them in an oval hoop instead. Similarly, some patterns lack grounding elements, but you can easily add some in if desired.

## Choosing Fabric Colors

The color of the fabric should complement the portrait colors—not compete with them. You may want to use a similar color for a more harmonious or monochromatic composition. Match the fabric to some of the pet's features such as their eye color or an undertone in their body.

Or, if you want to use complementary colors, choose a shade that is the opposite color of their fur, feathers, spines, or scales. For example, using a blue fabric will make orange fur appear extra vibrant.

Another option is to use the fabric to suggest a sense of environment. If you're creating a bird or fish portrait, you can use a shade of blue to suggest the sky or water. If you're stuck, you may find a white or off-white background is always a classic choice.

## Choosing a Display

Some embroidery artists like to keep their work in the embroidery hoop, and some like to have their work framed. It is just personal preference; there is no right or wrong way to display a piece. You may consider framing your piece with a square or rectangle frame to give the finished embroidery a different look.

# CREATING A PATTERN

## Drawing the Pattern

The most accurate way to capture the realism of a reference photo is to directly trace it. Avoid using any apps, programs, or filters to automatically generate an outline pattern for you. These programs usually miss key features, and the patterns hardly ever turn out well. You can also choose to freehand draw the pattern if you would like to create the portrait in your own style.

Whether you're creating your pattern digitally or traditionally, there are a few general steps you always need to take. First, size the reference photo to the size of your hoop, making sure you're aware of the scale you're stitching in so you don't trace out too many or too few details in the pattern. Larger hoops provide plenty of space to add extra details to your pattern.

Next, trace the outline of the pet and add in the facial features. Move on to tracing out any large contrasting areas of shadows, highlights, and color changes you see. You can also trace out any areas where you see movement in the coat if the animal has longer fur, feathers, or spines. After you've mapped out the larger and more obvious areas of color, work within each area to find smaller, more subtle shadows, highlights, and midtones. You can make these as detailed as you need. Try not to get overwhelmed with "seeing" and mapping out every color. This is something that will get easier with practice. Remember that all the projects in this book come with provided patterns.

Photo by Adam Wachtel & Susan Ussler

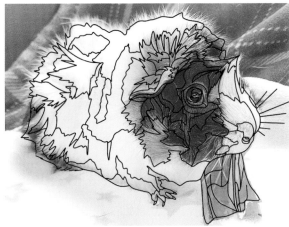

Pattern lines drawn over reference photo digitally

Final guinea pig pattern, scaled down

### DIGITALLY

Import the reference photo into your favorite drawing app, sized to your hoop. To draw the pattern on a separate layer, lower the opacity of the reference image so you can see your lines as you trace out the pattern. I like using a Wacom tablet with Adobe Photoshop or the Procreate app with my iPad and Apple Pencil. You can then print out the pattern and transfer it to the fabric (see Transferring a Pattern, page 22).

### TRADITIONALLY

Print out the reference photo after sizing it to your hoop. Tape it to a bright light source such as a window or lightbox and draw the pattern by tracing on a separate sheet of paper or tracing paper.

*tip* While you're stitching, it helps to have the reference photo on a device that allows you to zoom in and out to see the details. You can also have printed copies of the photo with different areas magnified if you can't use a device with a zoom feature.

## Stitch Paths

The most important part of creating a realistic-looking portrait is accurately capturing the natural directional flow of the fur, feathers, spines, scales, or body of the animal. Plan these stitch paths during your pattern drafting stage. Not only should your stitches follow the same direction of the fur, feathers, spines, and scales you see, but you should also keep in mind that those features can have different lengths across the body. For example, fur is generally shorter near the nose and eyes and gets longer as you move outward from the face. Reptiles and fish can have a different scale textures between their backs and their stomachs. Birds have different-size feathers throughout their bodies. This attention to small details brings out the realism in a portrait. For each pattern in this book, there is a dedicated stitch path direction guide. The ones pictured on this page include arrows for emphasis, while the stitch path guides in each project show the same feature with straight lines.

## CROSS CONTOUR LINES

Cross contour lines are similar to stitch paths and are used to give the embroidery more form and volume with your stitches. Cross contour lines can be horizontal or vertical and should be used in conjunction with the stitch path direction lines.

In the below examples, you can see that there is more volume to the snake with both horizontal and vertical cross contour lines, but the horizontal lines follow the natural direction of the body and scale pattern, so they should be the primary reference when stitching.

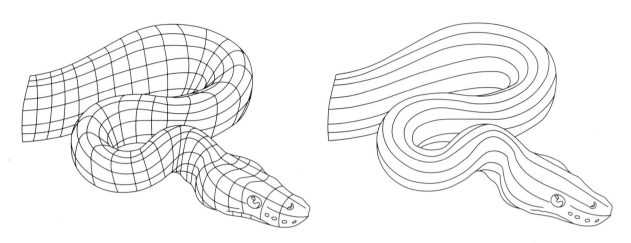

# TRANSFERRING A PATTERN

The patterns in this book have a lot of details and require precise lines; they therefore require a precise transfer onto fabric. After transferring the pattern, make sure the fabric is stretched drum-tight in the hoop, without any warping or stretching of the pattern.

## Pencils, Pens, or Markers

The most basic way of transferring an embroidery pattern is by using ordinary, everyday writing utensils such as a sharp pencil, pen, or marker. Tape the pattern to a bright window or lightbox and tape the fabric over it. Make sure the lines are precise, because the markings will be permanent unless you wash them out with a special fabric-stain remover.

### WATER-SOLUBLE FABRIC PENS

Water-soluble fabric pens are common and easy to find at most craft stores. Simply dampen the fabric, and the markings will disappear. Make sure the fabric is thoroughly washed and rinsed when finished or the lines can linger. Most water-soluble pens do not have a fine-enough tip to get all of the details for these patterns. Be sure to look for a fine-tip one!

### HEAT-ERASABLE PENS

You can use a heat-erasable FriXion pen (by Pilot) to trace out your pattern, and the markings will easily disappear with heat from an iron or a hair dryer. Mark lightly though, or faint lines will be left behind even after heat. These markings will also reappear in freezing temperatures and can leave bleach marks on denim or dark fabrics. I recommend using the 0.5mm extra fine-tip ones if you're choosing this method.

### WATER-SOLUBLE FABRIC STABILIZER

An easy way to transfer your pattern is by using a water-soluble fabric stabilizer. A common type is Sulky Fabri-Solvy Stabilizer. C&T Publishing Wash-Away Stitch Stabilizer also works the same way. You can either draw or print your pattern on the stabilizer and then adhere it to the fabric. Stitch directly on top of it. Once you're finished stitching, thoroughly soak the embroidery in water until the stabilizer dissolves.

*tip* **Some fabrics will shrink when washed. This can cause the embroidery to become wrinkled or puckered. You may want to wash the fabric before transferring the pattern if you are using a transferring method that requires washing.**

## Print

The most accurate way to transfer a digitally drawn pattern is to print it directly onto the fabric with your printer. Start by adhering a full sheet of sticker or label paper that fits in your printer to the wrong side of the fabric. Trim away any excess fabric. Then, print the pattern onto the fabric side. Peel off the sticker backing, and your fabric will have the pattern on it, ready for hooping. Run a hot iron over the pattern to set the color if you're using an inkjet printer. If you're using a laser printer with toner, pattern markings can be rubbed away as you stitch, so handle the fabric carefully while stitching.

*tip* **These options may not work for you if you are using a dark-colored fabric. In that case, use a fine-tip chalk pencil or white carbon paper to transfer the design.**

*Scan the QR code to view a video showing how I print patterns onto fabric!*

# THREAD PAINTING TECHNIQUES

## GETTING STARTED

Hoop the fabric drum-tight before you start stitching. Continue to adjust it as needed while you work. This will help prevent puckering around the stitches.

### Threading and Tying Off the Needle

Cut an arm's length piece of thread. Thread the needle, pulling the thread through so the tail end is about halfway down the length of the thread. Tie a small knot at the long end.

Begin stitching, holding the needle by the eye as much as you can while you work to prevent the thread tail from slipping out. Maintain the same thread ratio on either side of the needle, with one side half as long as the other, until there is only 1″–2″ (2.5–5cm) of thread left.

Then, tie the thread off and remove the needle. Tie off and remove the needle each time you change colors, saving longer thread scraps for later. To tie off the thread, bring the needle through to the back of the fabric and run it under a few of the previous stitches.

Then, bring the needle through the loop that's created, pulling it all the way through and securing the thread with a knot. It's okay if the back of the embroidery is a bit untidy or even really messy. To each their own!

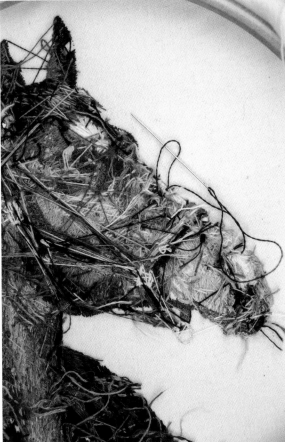

### Single-Strand Embroidery

The patterns in this book are primarily stitched with a single strand of thread. Most hand embroidery thread is stranded, meaning it consists of six strands of thread wrapped together. To separate the threads, start by trimming about an arm's length to use at a time. Then, while holding the end of the thread with one hand, pull a single strand out from the bunch. The thread will bunch up as you pull out the single strand but won't tangle once it's free.

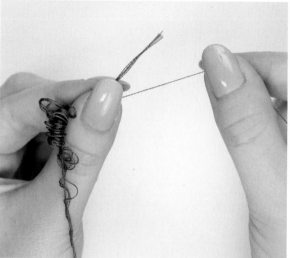

## THREAD PAINTING AND STITCHING TEXTURES

Thread painting, also known as needle painting, is an embroidery technique that uses long and short stitches to blend various colors and create a painterly effect. The placement of the stitches can result in different visual textures that range from silky smooth to coarse and choppy.

### Long and Short Stitch

Long and short stitch is a freeform style of stitching perfect for gradients and blending. I thread paint by making a wide range of stitch lengths, combining sets of long and short stitches. This gives a slightly unstructured look that mimics the shading in animal fur.

When you're thread painting with long and short stitch, an average stitch length should be about the size of a grain of rice, but it's important to make stitches of varying lengths. This will give more depth and texture to the embroidery. Using this stitching technique with only a single strand of thread makes color blending nearly seamless.

Use a No. 10 or 11 needle when thread painting with a single strand of thread because those needle sizes are the same width as the thread. Using a needle that's larger than the width of the thread will leave holes that the thread cannot fill. Use the eye of the needle or your fingernail to gently scratch over and close any holes you accidentally create with the needle.

If you use a needle that is smaller than the width of the thread, it will cause too much friction against the thread, making it appear fuzzy and eventually causing it to fray as you stitch.

## GRADIENT BLENDING

To blend long and short stitches, overlap them. Start each stitch by coming up through the previous ones, instead of ending by poking down into them from the top. Poking down into your stitches creates small needle holes in the thread.

You can create a simple gradient with just a few colors.

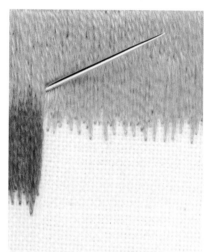 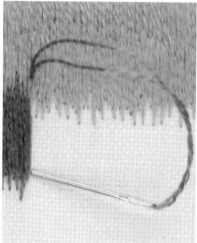 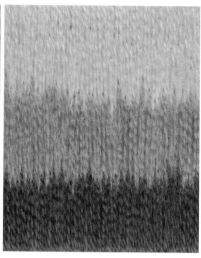

But the more colors you use, the more seamless the gradient will be. Add a color between each of the initial colors from the example above, and the look is much smoother. Make sure you are stitching in the same direction with each stitch.

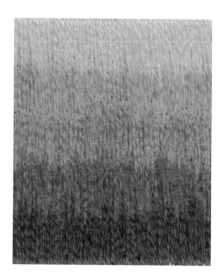

## TOP STITCHING

I refer to the process of stitching on top of previously stitched areas as *top stitching*. Top stitching is a way to emphasize the small hairs on an animal's face or the space between its scales, creating new lines or forms.

But you can also do what I call *top blending*. A traditional painter can combine two colors to create a third. This isn't possible with thread painting. Instead, you can stitch one color on top of another to change how the undertone looks, a process that tricks the eye into thinking the two colors are blended. You can also use this technique to add shading or highlights. Stitch an area of color, then add a blending color on top. Make sure you top stitch in the same direction as the original stitches.

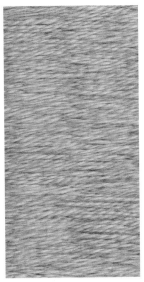

No top stitching

You can see how four stripes of top stitching added subtle color changes to the brown thread—in this example, a highlight, a shadow, and two changes in color tone.

### Quick Color Changes

Sometimes there are abrupt color changes in an animal's fur or feathers. To make these changes look more natural in embroidery, fill in each section of color separately. Then, top stitch with a third color over both sections to blend them together. Sometimes you may need to take this step even further, adding additional top stitching for highlights or shadows.

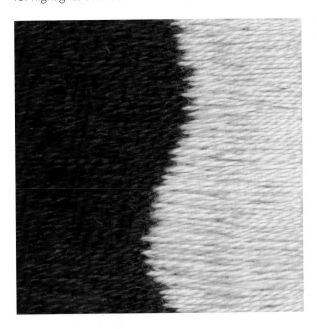

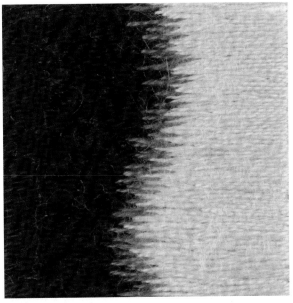

# CREATING TEXTURE

To practice with the textures in this project,
see Patterns (page 140).

## Fur

Fur can be tricky, as it can lay and stick out in a variety of ways that change the visual texture. It also varies greatly in length, color, and density.

Fur is not all one length. Vary the length of your long and short stitch to match the area of fur you're re-creating. As mentioned in Stitch Paths (page 20), the length of fur and size of feathers or scales can vary across the animal's body.

Stitch direction is also incredibly important. Focus on capturing the animal's natural contour lines with the direction of the stitches. Even if your color choices are a little off, the portrait will still end up looking lifelike if the stitch direction matches the look of the reference.

### STITCHING CURLY OR WAVY FUR

When thread painting an area of curly or wavy fur, make the stitches smaller as they go toward the inside of a curve. Stitch over previous stitches, and angle the stitches slightly to fill in a curved shape. It helps to make guidelines to follow and then fill in the interior curves.

## STITCHING STRAIGHT FUR

When there are overlapping sections of hair, work from the background to the foreground. In this example, I started with the white background, then moved to the outermost sections of fur. I moved to the middle sections of fur, and then I added the foreground last. The threads used in this example are 3866, 3865, White, 3033, 648, 434, 433, 435, 3827, 3021, 543, 3863, and 310.

I started with the white fur in the back, blending long and short stitches of 3866, 3865, White, and 3033. I top stitched some shadows with 648.

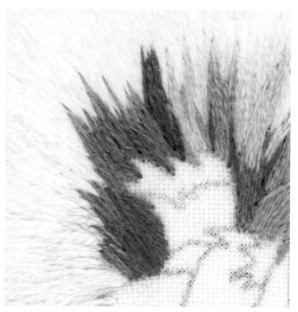

Next, I created the back section of brown-orange fur with 434, 433, and 435. I added highlights with 3827.

I stitched the front area of brown-orange fur with the same shades as the previous section, adding a shadow with 3021.

Finally, I filled in the remaining foreground section with 543, 3863, and 310.

## Feathers

The amount of detail you can add to feathers depends on how large the portrait is and what type of feathers the bird has. Bird feathers are typically smaller and more fur-like on the head and larger in the chest, wings, and tail. There is no need to stitch and define every single feather in the portrait for smaller birds. You can embroider a few to give the general idea that feathers are there, and thread paint the rest of the bird more generally.

This budgie has short feathers that appear fur-like. | Photo by Mary Hilton.

### STITCHING LARGE FEATHERS

A bird like a chicken has large and defined feathers on its chest. When you need to define feathers, use angled backstitches that meet in the middle, similar to the way you would embroider a leaf (see Easy Leaves, page 43). Start with the feathers at the bottom, and work your way up the bird's body. The threads used in this example are 938, 300, 975, 3371, 433, and 434.

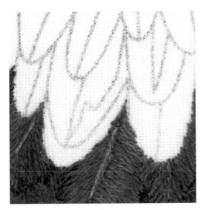

I used 938, 300, and 975 to create a bottom row of feathers. I accented between the feathers with 3371 for shadows. I used 433 and 434 to create the line down the middle of the feathers.

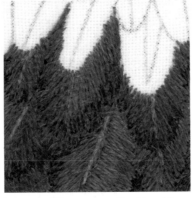

I repeated the same method to add a middle row of feathers.

Finally, I filled in the remaining feathers at the top.

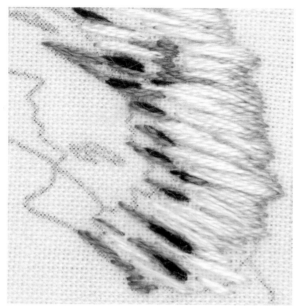

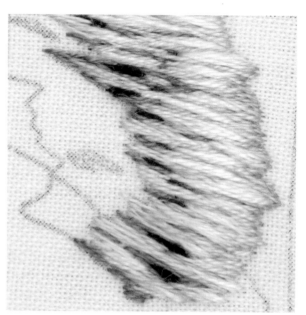

I added small shadows at the end of the spines with 646. I used 613 and 3865 to add the light tips of the quills. Then, I added 3371 and 611 to map out the small shadows between the quills. I staggered and overlapped each quill so they aren't all exactly the same.

I used 3782 and 613 to fill in the empty space around each quill, making the light tips of the quills stand out. I further defined the shadows with 611.

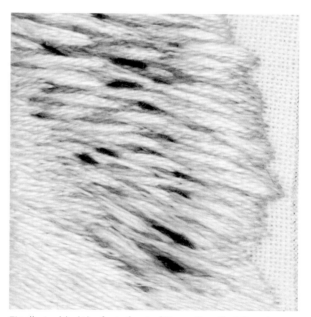

I repeated the same method to create the next section of quills. I defined the darker shadows with 3371 and mapped out the direction of new quills with 611. I added more quill tips with 3865, making sure to overlap them with the previous section. I added 613 and 3782 to negative space and for shadow.

Finally, I added the fur in front of the quills with 648 and 3866. For the lighter fur in the bottom left corner, I used 3866 and top stitched with White.

## Scales

Scales are all about texture and pattern. They can be either horizontal or vertical, depending on the pose of the animal and the natural contour lines (see Cross Contour Lines, page 21).

### Brick Stitch

Use a brick stitch to create scales. A brick stitch is a simple backstitch worked in offset rows. This gives the same patterning as a brick wall. I suggest working in horizontal rows to keep the stitch even. Brick stitch does not have to be perfect; the eye will naturally see patterns. It can even be helpful to have multiple needles threaded with each color that you need for a section. Leave them tucked into the fabric when they're not in use, then untangle the correct color as needed.

Since you are working with a set pattern in the brick stitch, there isn't room to capture every shade of color—you won't be blending colors like you would when thread painting. So simplify the coloring to fit within the stitch pattern. You can still top stitch over and around the stitches to give the idea of shadows and highlights and to blend color sections.

## STITCHING SCALES

When creating scales, I like to stitch over each brick stitch two to three times to give it more volume, which I call a *stacked brick stitch*. Stacking two strands of thread gives you more control over the brick stitch, especially around the edges of the animal where the brick stitch may be smaller or cut off. The threads used in this example are 3033, 3782, 3790, 3799, 08, 3863, 413, 04, and 310.

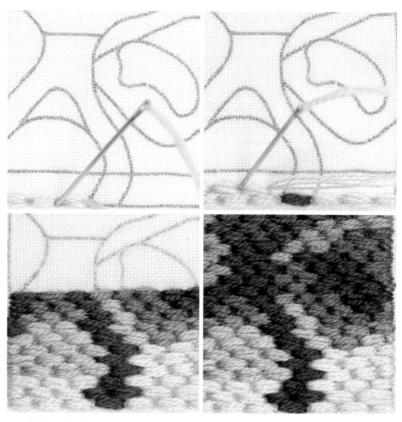

I worked row by row with two strands of thread and brick stitch, using colors 3033, 3782, 3790, 3799, 08, 3863, and 413 to create the snake's scales.

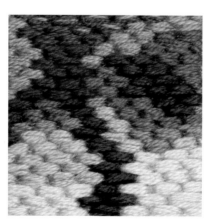

I used single strands of 04 and 310 to create small shadows and highlights on top of the scales. I stitched the shadows near the bottom of a row and the highlights near the top.

*tip* **Blend brick stitch by using small top stitches over the area you wish to blend. Make sure to follow the same brick stitch pattern with the top stitches. This will trick the eye and make the colors appear blended.**

# CHOOSING COLORS

The pressure of choosing the right color is often daunting. Thankfully, it's something that gets easier with time and practice. The more experience you have, the easier it will be to match a color to thread.

One way to make this easier is to reference a color chart from the brand of thread you're using. I like the DMC color chart made with real thread. The colors are grouped into smaller color families and go from light to dark. Reference those color palettes and then pull in colors from other families as needed.

*tip* **You can adjust the warm or cool tones of your reference photo and change the contrast as needed to make the colors look truer to life.**

If you're able to shop for embroidery thread in person, take your reference photo with you. Hold the thread up to the photo and compare colors.

Begin with the most prevalent color in the reference photo, and locate either the darkest or lightest color within that hue range. Match those colors first. Then move to smaller areas of other colors, such as the eyes and nose, and choose colors for those areas. As you identify colors, create gradients around them for the shadows and highlights. Remember, the more colors in a gradient, the smoother the blending will be.

You can also use cross-stitch pattern generators to help you choose colors. These generators will turn your photo into a cross-stitch pattern with corresponding thread colors. The guides aren't always completely accurate, and cross-stitch does not require the same amount of gradient detail as thread painting, but they give you a place to start and a general color family to explore.

Some colors appear different on the skein than they do in the embroidery. If you are unfamiliar with the color palette you're using, do some test blending on a scrap piece of fabric before starting on a portrait. Make sure you are stitching in even-toned lighting or natural daylight to accurately see the colors.

# PORTRAIT ACCENTS

Give your portrait a bit of flair by adding some extra embroidered accents. You might add the pet's name, an important date, or some flowers and other greenery.

# NAMES AND DATES

Personalize your portrait by adding the pet's name or a significant date. Use your own handwriting or the letter patterns (see Patterns, page 142) to write out the name. A split backstitch is great for creating delicate lettering.

To create a split backstitch, bring the needle up at point A and then back down at point B, and then repeat at C and D. Continue stitching, repeating the process and ensuring that the stitch back down (C to D) slightly overlaps the previous stitch.

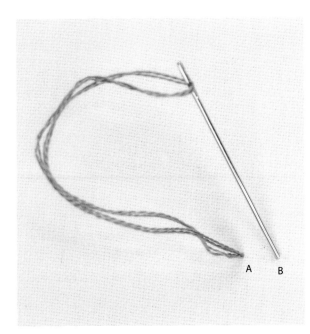
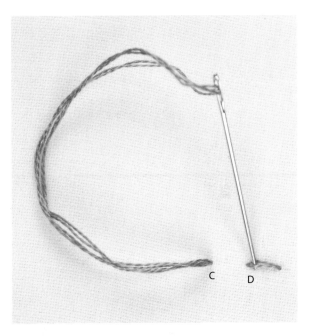

For cursive letters, use small split backstitches to create the curves in the letters. The tighter the curve in the letter, the shorter the stitches should be. Use a single strand of thread for an even neater finish.

# FLORAL ACCENTS

With just a few simple stitches, you can create a whole array of different flowers. Practice with the shapes in this book (see Patterns, page 141) or come up with your own combinations! Add flowers around your portraits as decoration.

## Satin Stitch Flowers and Leaves

You can create almost any flower or leaf with a simple satin stitch. Using one or two strands of thread, bring the needle up at point A and down at point B, and then again at points C and D. Continue filling in the flower petals by working from the outer edge of each petal toward the center. Fill each petal, then fill in the center of the flower with more satin stitch or even French knots (page 42)!

*tip* Use the stitching techniques in Thread Painting Techniques (page 24) for to create flowers that look more realistic, adding shadows and highlights.

Examples of satin stitch florals. Floral pattern illustrations provided by Paulo Rezende.

## Woven Roses

To start a woven rose, with a pencil, draw a circle split into even fifths. Using six strands of thread, make a single long backstitch on each of the lines through the circle, creating spokes that go to the outside of the circle and meet in the middle.

Using 6 or more strands of thread, bring the needle up through the fabric next to the center. Then, skipping a spoke, weave the needle under the next spoke, making sure you don't poke the needle through the fabric or the spokes. Weave the needle over and under every other spoke, moving outward until you've completed the rose and the spokes are completely covered. Turn the hoop as you work if you need a better angle. Don't pull the thread so tight that the rose gets warped. Continue weaving the thread through the spokes until they're fully covered.

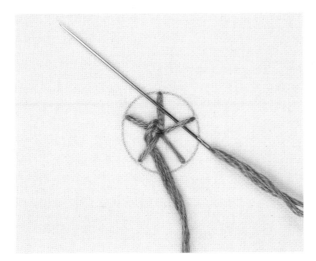
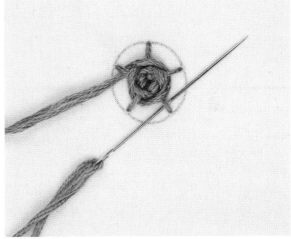

To finish the rose, bring the needle back through the fabric on the edge of the rose and tie it off behind the hoop. Make the rose extra fluffy by using the needle to lightly separate each section of petals.

## French Knots

French knots can be used as filler between other floral elements or as florals themselves! They also provide texture in many of the projects. The more strands of thread you use, the larger the French knot will be.

Using 2 strands of thread, bring the needle up through the fabric. Wrap the thread around the shaft of the needle 2–4 times. Bring the needle back down into the fabric right next to where you originally came up while still holding the working thread. Slide the wrapped thread around the needle down to the fabric. Pull the needle all the way through to secure the French knot in place.

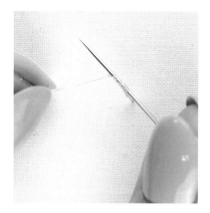 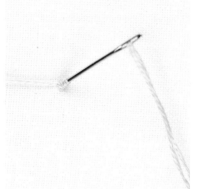 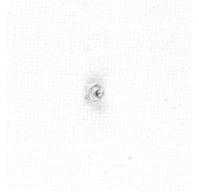

French knot florals

## LEAFY ACCENT WREATH

Use a combination of a split backstitch and an angled backstitch to create the leaves in this leafy wreath. Add some berries or small flowers with French knots as additional embellishment. If your pet doesn't fit in the center of the wreath, you can overlap the two elements in the foreground. Leave some gaps between the leaves, and add satin stitch flowers for an extra decorative accent. See Patterns, page 141.

### Easy Leaves

To make a single leaf, split the leaf shape down the center and fill in one half with angled backstitches. Fill in the second half of the leaf with the same stitch, mirrored, from the outside to the inside so that the stitches meet in the center. Vary this leaf shape by adding veining, or varying the angle of the stitches.

You can make these leaves more detailed by adding shading with thread painting. You can also use this leaf shape to make feathers (Creating Texture, page 30).

# FINISHING THE HOOP

# BACKING THE HOOP

There are multiple ways to finish the back of an embroidery hoop, but I suggest avoiding any that use glue. Glue isn't always archival, so it can discolor the fabric over time. Embroidery fabric tension can also loosen over time, and if you use glue, you cannot readjust the tension of the fabric.

To finish a hoop with thread, trim the outer fabric down to about 1″ (2.5cm) around the hoop. Before doing this, make sure the embroidery is centered in the hoop and that the fabric is pulled taut and free of wrinkles.

Using two strands of thread, weave the needle in and out of the fabric around the outside of the hoop. This is called a running stitch. Make sure to stitch through both layers of fabric if you are using multiple layers in your hoop. Do this along the outside edge of the fabric.

Pull tight at the end to cinch in the fabric. Tie off the thread to secure. You can leave the back open or cover it with felt or another piece of fabric.

# FRAMING AND DISPLAYING

One simple way to elevate your finished embroidery is to frame it. You can buy a frame specifically made to fit embroidery hoops or take the embroidery to have it professionally framed. Choose a frame color and shape that will accent the portrait.

Show off the artwork by hanging it on a wall or by placing it on a shelf, bookcase, or table. Avoid displaying it in bright direct sunlight or in an area with moisture.

# FUR, FEATHERS, SPINES, AND SCALES
# THREAD PAINTED PORTRAITS

EACH PORTRAIT PROJECT IN THIS BOOK HAS A PROVIDED PATTERN (SEE PATTERNS, PAGE 140). ADDITIONALLY, EACH PROJECT HAS A COLOR GUIDE SHOWING WHICH COLORS ARE USED WITHIN THE PATTERN. ALL COLOR NUMBERS CORRESPOND TO DMC THREAD COLORS UNLESS OTHERWISE STATED. THE COLOR GUIDES ARE APPROXIMATE AND DO NOT SHOW EVERY STITCH OF COLOR BUT INSTEAD GIVE A GENERAL IDEA OF HOW THE COLORS WILL FILL IN THE PATTERN. BETWEEN FOLLOWING THE STEP-BY-STEP PHOTOS AND REFERENCING THE COLOR GUIDES, YOU WILL BE ABLE TO CREATE YOUR VERY OWN EMBROIDERED ANIMAL PORTRAITS BASED ON THESE PATTERNS.

These projects can be challenging. As you work, you may find yourself getting frustrated with one part and wish to move to a different section. You may also notice things you forgot to add to a previous area or see something you wish to change. This is okay, and it's fine to bounce around to different areas of the portrait, as long as it doesn't interrupt the flow from the background to the foreground of the figure.

Creating a realistic portrait requires a hefty range of thread colors and is not an inexpensive endeavor. Patterns in this book use anywhere from 13 to 45 colors each. You will need 148 different colors total to accurately stitch every pattern provided. You might just discover that, through purchasing all the different thread colors you need to complete each portrait here, you have all the thread you'll need for future portraits. Unless otherwise stated, stitch using a single strand of thread.

Some portraits have patterns that extend all the way to the edge of the hoop. To accomplish this, you will need to position your design off-center in the hoop so your needle can reach the edge of the pattern. You can also use a larger embroidery hoop while stitching and then finish the portrait in a smaller hoop once it's complete. Note that all references to *right* and *left* in the instructions refers to the image as it appears in the hoop, not the animal in real life.

# Rabbit | *Hops*

**THIS PATTERN SPENDS A LOT OF TIME WITH THE SHADOWS AND HIGHLIGHTS OF THE RABBIT'S FUR** and is easily customizable. Swap out the black and gray tones for brown, or add a fur pattern to make the bunny look like one of your own! This pattern was stitched on Kona Cotton in the color White. Use the Rabbit Pattern (page 140) to prepare the hoop.

Photo by Ashley Danh

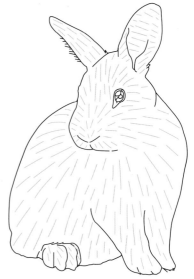

Stitch direction guide

## THREAD COLORS

| | | | |
|---|---|---|---|
| ■ | 04 | ■ | 3787 |
| ■ | 535 | □ | WHITE |
| ■ | 3799 | ■ | 224 |
| ■ | 310 | ■ | 3859 |
| ■ | 336 | ■ | 3861 |
| ■ | 3371 | ■ | 632 |

*NOTE: Additionally, Gütermann 9045 is used to stitch the whiskers and eyebrows.*

*Did you know?*
*Rabbits are highly intelligent and can be trained like dogs.*

Color guide

1 Reference the color guide, and fill in the back foot and the stomach with 310, 3799, 535, and 04. Work from darkest colors to lightest in this area.

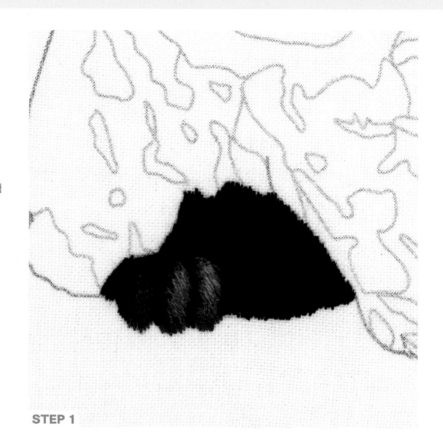

**STEP 1**

2 Stitch the front legs with 310, 3799, 535, and 04. Use small top stitches as needed to blend the colors.

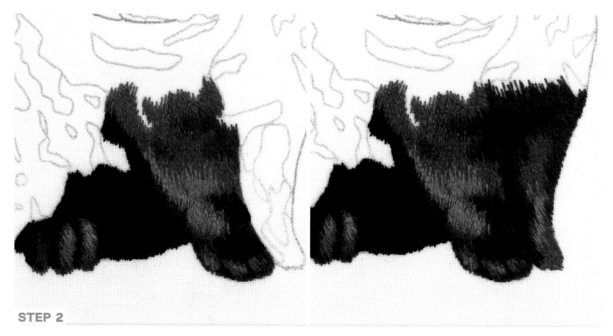

**STEP 2**

**3** Fill in the right side of the rabbit's chest and shoulder with 310, 3799, 535, and 04, making sure to follow the curve in the stitch direction guide.

STEP 3

**4** Using the same colors as Step 3, move to the left shoulder and back, under the rabbit's head. Use a lot of small top stitches of 310 and 3799 to make the rabbit's fur appear dense and short. Then, finish the back by moving downward toward the back foot.

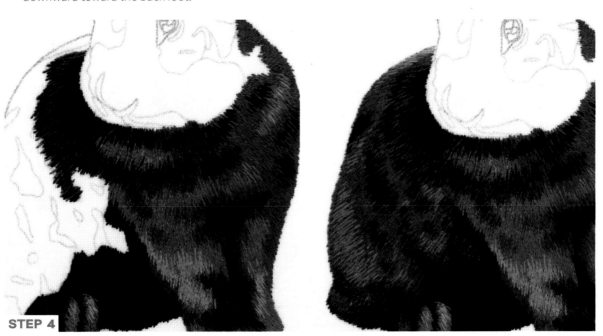

STEP 4

**5** Move to the rabbit's eye. Use 310 and 336 for the pupil and 3787 to create the iris around the top of the pupil. Fill in the rest of the iris with 3371. Add highlights in the eye with 04 and White. Use 3861 for the area of skin around the eye as shown.

STEP 5

**6** Using 310, 3799, 535, and 04, fill in the face around the mouth and work your way outward and upward all the way to the top of the head.

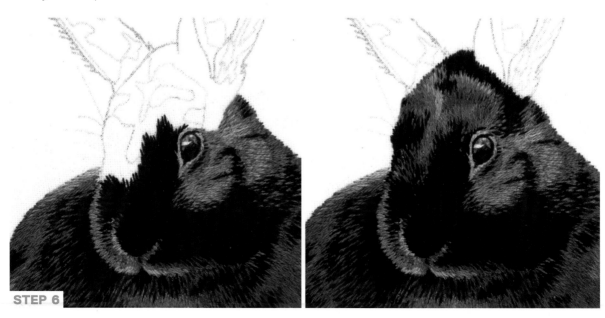

STEP 6

**7** Stitch the right ear with 632, 3859, 224, 3799, and 3371. Start with the inner ear, then add the dark black fur of the outer ear. Top stitch 3371 between 632 and the 310 at the top of the head to blend the 2 sections around the top curve of the ear. Use a few top stitches of 3799 to blend the pink of the ear into the black fur near the lower portion of the ear.

**8** Start the second ear by stitching the small outer ear hairs with 3799. Then, fill in the rest of the ear with 310, 3799, 535, and 04.

STEP 7

STEP 8

**9** Finish the portrait by stitching the whiskers and eyebrows with a split backstitch (see Portrait Accents, page 39) in Gütermann 9045.

*tip* **If a pet has white whiskers that look too jarring against darker fur when stitched, use a light gray or beige thread color instead. This will make the contrast less harsh.**

STEP 9

# Hamster | *Madame Fluffypants*

**THIS HAMSTER IS CURIOUS AND SWEET,** with a lifted paw that makes it look like it might walk out of the hoop. If you want it to look like your own hamster, just swap out thread colors I chose for her blonde fur with those that match your furry friend. This pattern was stitched on Kona Cotton in the color White. Use the Hamster Pattern (page 140) to prepare the hoop.

Photo by Brenda Snyman, Tiny Toes Animal Photography

Stitch direction guide

**THREAD COLORS**

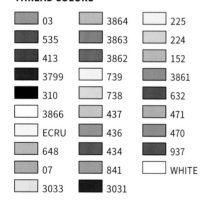

| | | |
|---|---|---|
| 03 | 3864 | 225 |
| 535 | 3863 | 224 |
| 413 | 3862 | 152 |
| 3799 | 739 | 3861 |
| 310 | 738 | 632 |
| 3866 | 437 | 471 |
| ECRU | 436 | 470 |
| 648 | 434 | 937 |
| 07 | 841 | WHITE |
| 3033 | 3031 | |

*NOTE: Additionally, White Gütermann is used to stitch the whiskers.*

Color Guide

*Did you know?*
*There are about twenty species of hamster but only a few types have been domesticated.*

**1** If you want to include the wreath accent, start by stitching it first. Stitch the wreath and branches with one strand of 434 and a split backstitch (see Portrait Accents, page 39). Then, use two strands of thread to create the leaves with 471, 470, and 937. Finish the wreath by adding little French knots with 3866 and two strands of thread on the branch ends.

STEP 1

**2** Begin the hamster portrait by stitching the feet and toes. Use 632 between the toes and for the first two toes on the back foot. Then use 3861, 225, and 224 to fill in the rest of the feet.

**3** Fill in the backside of the hamster's body with 437 and 738. Add a shadow along the lower tummy near the feet with 07.

**STEP 2**

**STEP 3**

**4** Fill in the next section of the back with 738, 739, and 436. Add highlights in the fur with ECRU.

**5** Stitch the fur on the lower stomach between and above the front paws with 3862, 3863, 3864, 841, and 436.

**STEP 4**

**STEP 5**

**6** Fill in the lower left side of the body and chest with 437 and 738.

**STEP 6**

**7** Add the fur on the chest under the chin with 436, 437, and 3864. Keep the stitches short to blend them easily.

**STEP 7**

**8** Stopping near the eyes, fill in the left and right sides of the face, around the snout. Use 738, ECRU, and 3864. Add 3033 under the eyes.

STEP 8

**9** Use 632 and 3861 to stitch the mouth, and then add the chin fur with White and ECRU. Add a few top stitches of 3864 to blend the fur into the lower lip.

STEP 9

**10** Fill in the nostrils with 632. Then use 224 for the lower area of the nose, 152 for the upper area of nose, and 225 to add highlights.

Outline the eyes with 310, and then add a highlight on the outer edges of each eye with 413. Use 03 to make the highlights in the eyes, and then fill in the rest of the eyes with 310. Add a White highlight on top of the 03 stitches, then use 3799 for the upper and lower eyelids.

**11** Start the hamster's cheeks by stitching the area of skin around the nose with 3861. Add a line down the center of the cheeks, around and below the nose, with 632. Fill in the cheek fur with 739, and then use 3033 to blend the fur into the area of skin. Add an area of white along the bottom of the cheeks with White and then add a few highlights up the sides of the cheeks with the same color.

STEP 10

STEP 11

**12** Stitch the ears with 3031, 3799, and a few top stitches of 535.

**13** Fill in the top of the forehead with 738, 3864, and 739. Use ECRU above the eyes. Add tufts of fur above the ears with 648 and 3033.

STEP 12

STEP 13

**14** For the remaining middle of the face, use 3033, White, 738, ECRU, and 437.

STEP 14

**15** Finish the portrait by stitching the whiskers with a split backstitch (see Portrait Accents, page 39) in White Gütermann.

STEP 15

# Guinea Pig | *Miru*

**I CHOSE TO STITCH THIS GUINEA PIG'S PORTRAIT ON PINK FABRIC** to accent her orange fur and highlight her white fur. She's nibbling on a snack—a lettuce leaf! This pattern was stitched on Kona Cotton in the color Bellini. Use the Guinea Pig Pattern (page 140) to prepare the hoop.

Photo by Adam Wachtel & Susan Ussler

**THREAD COLORS**

| | | | | |
|---|---|---|---|---|
| WHITE | 413 | 3371 | 224 | 3348 |
| 3865 | 3799 | 3827 | 3779 | 524 |
| 3866 | 310 | 437 | 3861 | 523 |
| 648 | 05 | 436 | 3859 | 470 |
| 3033 | 3782 | 435 | 3064 | 3347 |
| 3021 | 543 | 434 | 3747 | 904 |
| 03 | 3864 | 433 | 827 | 937 |
| 317 | 3863 | 801 | 3750 | 3345 |
| 535 | 3862 | 225 | 823 | |

*NOTE: Additionally, Gütermann 9045 is used to stitch the whiskers.*

Stitch direction guide

Color guide

*Did you know?*
*Some guinea pigs have hair swirls called rosettes.*

1. Reference the color guide, and fill in the guinea pig's backside with 310 and 3799. Next, use 3865, 648, 05, 3866, and 3782 to create the area of light-colored fur next to the first section. Work from the lower left toward the upper right of the body so the stitches overlap and mimic the look of the guinea pig's fur.

2. Fill in the upper backside area with 3866, 3865, and White.

STEP 1

STEP 2

3. Fill in the lower tummy and arm with 05, 3865, 648, and White. Create the paw and toes with 3779, 3861, and 3064.

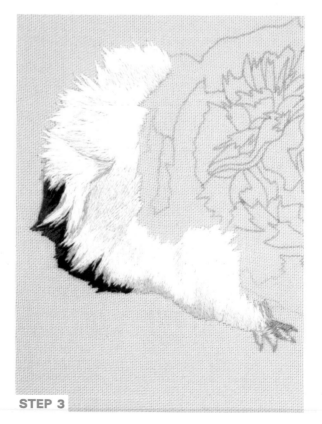

STEP 3

**4** Fill in the remaining area of the back with 3033, 3866, 648, and White. Use 3782 to create some shadows in the gaps in the fur.

STEP 4

**5** Moving to the forehead, work from the fur in the background to the fur in the foreground with 310, 3799, 317, 435, White, 648, 3033, 434, 433, 3021, 3827, and 801. See Stitching Straight Fur (page 32) for an example of stitching from background to foreground. Use 3863 for the small piece of visible ear on the right edge of the portrait.

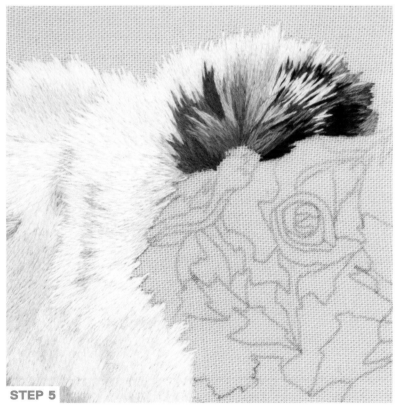

STEP 5

**6** Starting at the top of the left ear and moving toward the tip, stitch with 3862, 3863, 3864, 543, 434, and 3371. The ear stitches should look smoother and flatter than the fur above the ear.

Use 310 to fill in most of the iris and pupil in the eye. Use 3799 to highlight the top of the iris. Add some blue around the pupil with 823 and 3750. Add highlights with 827, 03, and White. Use 535 for the skin around the eye.

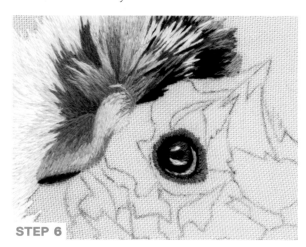

STEP 6

**7** Fill in the area above the eye and the upper cheek with 310, 413, 3799, 433, 3021, 434, 436, and 3747. Work from the inner face outward.

STEP 7

**8** Move to the lettuce leaf. Fill it in with 937, 3348, 3347, 523, 904, 524, 470, and 3345. Work from the top of the leaf down and then add the leaf veins.

*tip* **You can choose to omit the lettuce leaf, or replace it with some other snack if you'd like.**

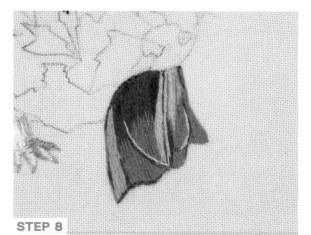

STEP 8

**9** Stitch the lower portion of the face and the cheek to the left of the nose with 05, 3865, 434, 3021, 436, 310, 3799, and 413.

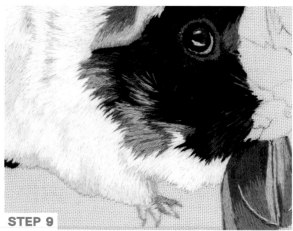

STEP 9

**10** Use 3859 to create the nostril, and then fill in 224 and 225 around it. Fill in the rest of the lower snout with 648, 437, 3865, and 3033.

Fill in the area above the nose, leading to the forehead, with 3866, 3033, 3799, 648, 3782, 535, and 436. Overlap the stitches above the nose with the start of the swooping tuft of hair at the top of the head.

**STEP 10**

**11** Finish the portrait by stitching the whiskers with a split backstitch (see Portrait Accents, page 39) in Gütermann 9045.

**STEP 11**

# Rat | *Boonie*

**THIS RAT HAS BOTH WARM AND COOL GRAY TONES IN HIS FUR,** so the pattern requires a lot of top stitching to blend them together. Pay close attention to the top stitching lines on the color guide. Notice that you don't have to stitch the entire reference photo, and this portrait stops below the front paws. This pattern was stitched on Kona Cotton in the color Natural. Use the Rat Pattern (page 140) to prepare the hoop.

Photo by Brenda Snyman,
Tiny Toes Animal Photography

Stitch direction guide

## THREAD COLORS

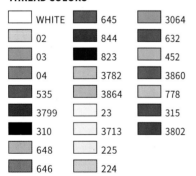

| | | |
|---|---|---|
| WHITE | 645 | 3064 |
| 02 | 844 | 632 |
| 03 | 823 | 452 |
| 04 | 3782 | 3860 |
| 535 | 3864 | 778 |
| 3799 | 23 | 315 |
| 310 | 3713 | 3802 |
| 648 | 225 | |
| 646 | 224 | |

*NOTE: Additionally, Gütermann White is used to stitch the whiskers and eyebrows*

*Did you know?*
*Rats have an incredible sense of smell and can be trained to sniff out illnesses.*

Color guide

1   Reference the color guide, and begin the portrait in the bottom left corner on the rat's tummy. Stitch with 03, 646, 04, 645, and 02, stopping by the armpit. Do more top stitching than normal to capture the rat's mousy gray fur.

2   Continue working your way to the right by filling in the center of the rat's tummy with 02, 03, 646, 04, and 648.

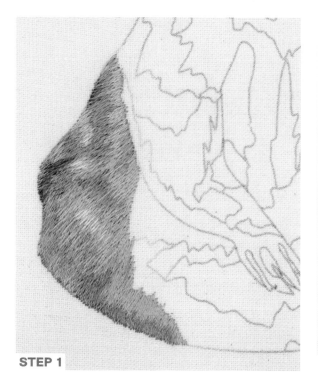

STEP 1

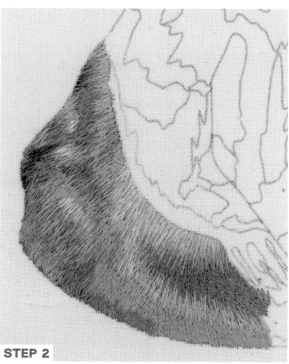

STEP 2

3   Fill in the remaining lower right side with 646, 03, 02, 04, and 645.

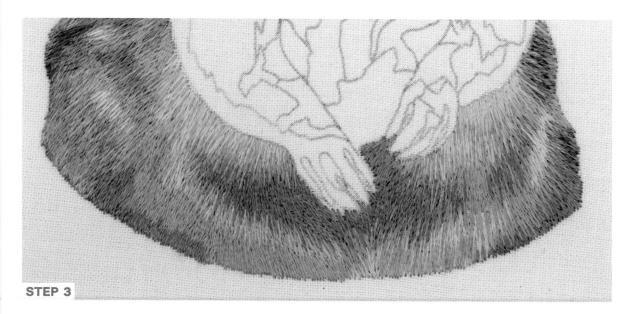

STEP 3

**4** Using 02, 03, 04, 646, 645, and 844, begin filling in the middle of the rat's chest, working from the chin downward. Start with the darker colors and work your way to the lighter ones, top stitching as needed to blend. Pay close attention to the stitch direction.

*tip* You can use 535 to top stitch shadows near the inner arms here in Step 4 or later in Step 6.

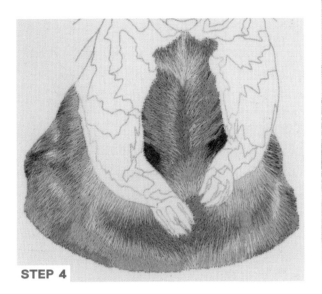

**STEP 4**

**5** Fill in the rat's paws with 632, 224, 23, and 225.

**STEP 5**

**6** Starting at the left shoulder and working down toward the hand, stitch the left arm with 04, 03, 844, 645, 646, 648, 02, and 3799. Fill in the right arm with the same colors as the left arm.

If you did not add enough shadow to the rat's chest and armpits with 535 in Step 4, do so now.

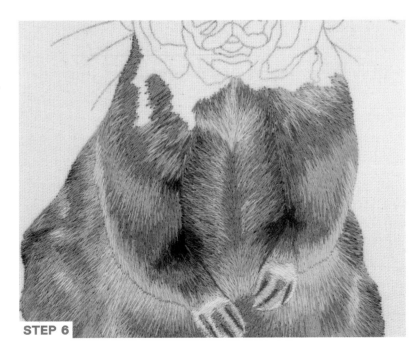

**STEP 6**

**7** Starting at the top of the rat's ears and working downward, stitch with 3064, 3864, and 452. Top stitch to blend each area of color into the next.

Use 310 to fill in the pupil and iris of the eyes. Add a blue reflection around the outer edge of each eye with 823. Use 03 to create curved highlights in the eyes, and accent them with White. Use 535 above and below each eye for the eyelids.

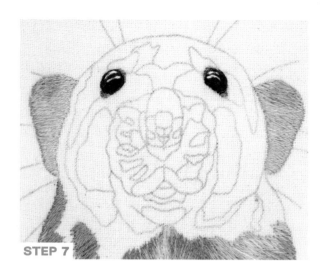

STEP 7

**8** Beginning under the chin and working upward, fill in the left side of the face with 02, 03, 04, and 535.

**9** Continue across the forehead and down the right side of the face with the same colors used in Step 8.

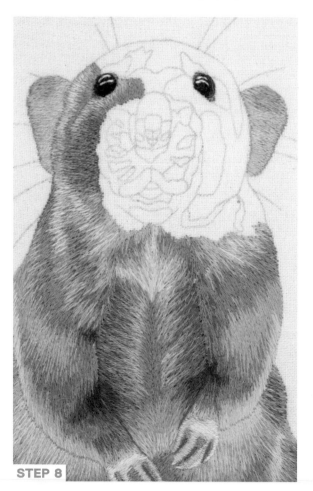

STEP 8

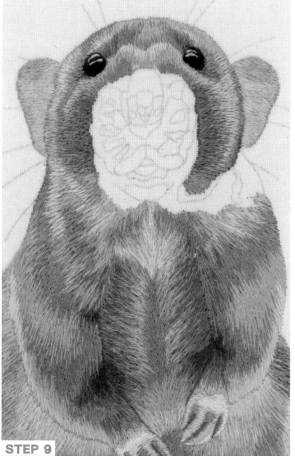

STEP 9

**10** Stitch the rat's tooth with 3782, and then fill in the chin and remaining neck under the chin with 02, 03, 844, 535, 04, and 646.

Create the pink nose with 3802, 315, 778, 3860, and 3713. Fill in the area above the nose with 645, 646, 03, and 02.

**11** Using 645, 646, 04, 03, and 648, fill in the left and right cheeks. Work from the center of the cheeks outward toward the edges.

STEP 10

STEP 11

**12** Finish the portrait by stitching the whiskers and eyebrows with a split backstitch (see Portrait Accents, page 39) in Gütermann White.

STEP 12

# Ferret | *Bob*

**THIS PATTERN CALLS FOR A LOT OF TOP STITCHING TO BLEND THE FERRET'S FUR.** Make sure to follow the color guide closely as you stitch. This pattern was stitched on Kona Cotton in the color Suede. Use the Ferret Pattern (page 140) to prepare the hoop.

Photo by Sandy Entrena Ramos

Stitch direction guide

## THREAD COLORS

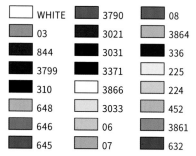

| | | |
|---|---|---|
| WHITE | 3790 | 08 |
| 03 | 3021 | 3864 |
| 844 | 3031 | 336 |
| 3799 | 3371 | 225 |
| 310 | 3866 | 224 |
| 648 | 3033 | 452 |
| 646 | 06 | 3861 |
| 645 | 07 | 632 |

*NOTE: Additionally, Gütermann 2960 or a dark gray-brown thread is used to stitch the whiskers and eyebrows.*

## *Did you know?*

*A group of ferrets is called a business.*

Color guide

1 Reference the color guide, and begin the portrait on the right side of the neck. Stitch with 310, 3790, 3371, and 3021, stopping under the neck. Work from the darker colors to the lighter colors, top stitching as needed to blend.

2 Moving toward the center of the chest, use the same colors from Step 1, making sure to blend with a lot of top stitching using 310.

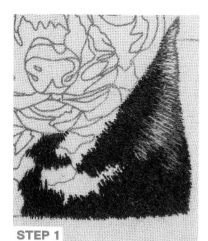

STEP 1

STEP 2

3 Finish the left side of the neck with 3371, 310, 3021, 645, 646, and 648.

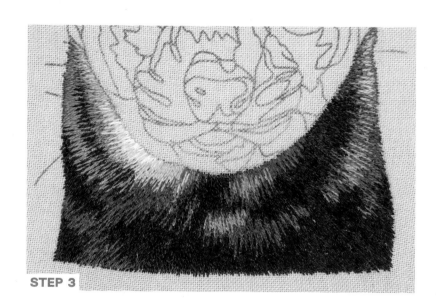

STEP 3

4 Fill the middle of the eyes with 310. Then, add a blue accent with 336 and a subtle highlight with 3799 to each eye. Add brighter highlights with 03 and White to each eye. Stitch the skin around both eyes with 452 and 3861.

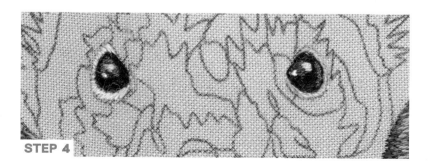

STEP 4

**5** Fill in the nostrils and below the nose with 632. Add shadows to the nostrils with 3031. Use 3861, 225, and 224 to fill in the rest of the nose.

**6** On the chin, stitch 844 near the center of the mouth, and then use 224, 646, 645, 648, and White to finish the rest of the space.

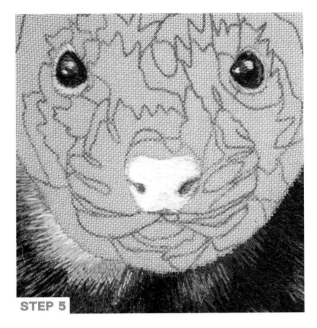

STEP 5

STEP 6

**7** Stitch the cheeks one at a time, working from the bottom up with overlapping stitches. Use 646, 648, White, 07, and 06 on the left cheek, and 648, 646, 07, and White on the right cheek.

**8** Use 225, 07, White, and 648 to fill the area above the nose.

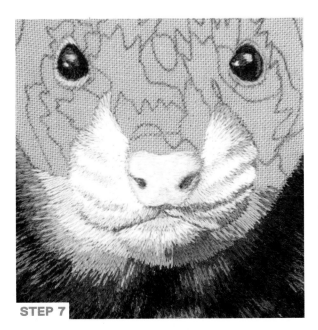

STEP 7

STEP 8

**9** Stitch the area around the left eye and side of the face with 3031, 452, 225, 3033, 08, 3371, 646, 3864, and 645. Keep the stitches small in this area to help blend all of the colors.

STEP 9

**10** Fill in the center of the face, between the eyes, with 08, 646, 3866, and 3371.

STEP 10

**11** Stitch around the right eye with 3861, 3371, 3031, 3790, 645, 844, 648, 646, and 08. Continue using short stitches to blend.

STEP 11

**12** Stitch the inner left ear with 224, 3864, and 3861. Stitch the top of the ear with 3866 and 648. Stitch the hairs in front of the ear and near the base of the ear with 645, 646, and 648.

For the right ear, stitch with 3861 for the inner pink area, and then use 3866, 648, and 646 for the top of the ear. Use 844, 3371, 646, and 645 to stitch the fur in front of the ear and at the base of the ear.

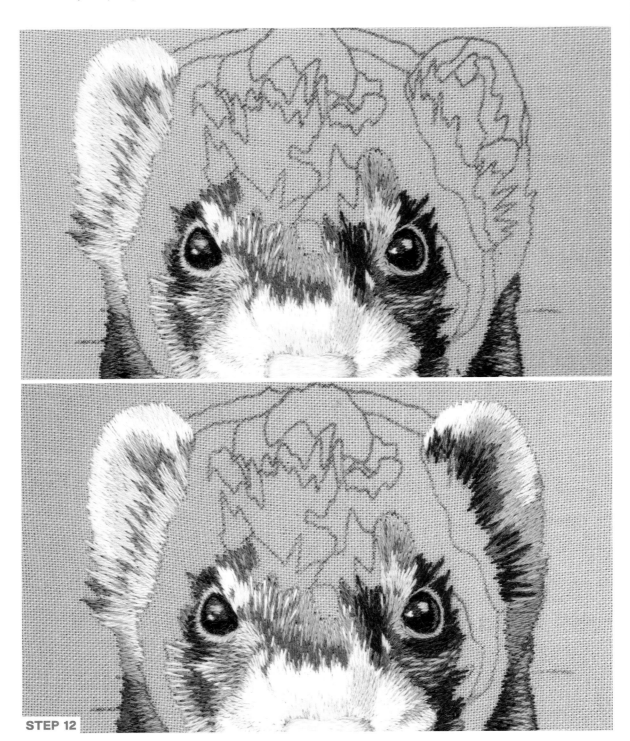

STEP 12

**13** Fill in the forehead and across the top of the head with 648, 07, 646, 3864, 3866, White, 3033, 844, and 3371.

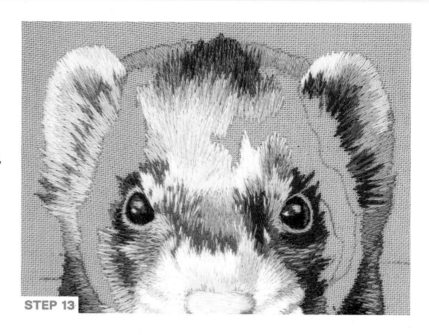

STEP 13

**14** Stitch the remaining left side of the face with 3033, White, 648, and 3864. Repeat, stitching the right side with 3033, 648, 08, 646, 3371, and 3866.

STEP 14

**15** Finish the portrait by stitching the whiskers and eyebrows with a split backstitch (see Portrait Accents, page 39) in dark gray-brown thread or Gütermann 2960.

STEP 15

# Hedgehog | *Chonky*

**THE HEDGEHOG'S QUILLS CAN BE VERY INTIMIDATING.** Take your time and work in small sections. I've given the hedgehog both grounding and background elements since it's a full-body portrait. This pattern was stitched on Kona Cotton in the color Eucalyptus. Use the Hedgehog Pattern (page 140) to prepare the hoop.

@chonkythehedgehog | Photo by Taylor Wong

Stitch direction guide

**THREAD COLORS**

| | | |
|---|---|---|
| WHITE | 613 | 3371 |
| 04 | 611 | 471 |
| 535 | 07 | 3347 |
| 3799 | 08 | 3051 |
| 310 | 648 | 640 |
| 3865 | 645 | 3787 |
| 3866 | 3021 | 800 |
| 822 | 3864 | 336 |
| 3782 | 3862 | 224 |
| 3790 | 3033 | 451 |
| 3031 | 646 | |

*NOTE: Additionally, Gütermann 2960 or a dark gray-brown thread is used to stitch the whiskers.*

Color guide

*Did you know?*

*Hedgehogs can swim.*

1. Reference the color guide, and stitch the shadow under the hedgehog with 3787 and 640. Next, skipping the blades of grass that intersect the hedgehog, stitch the rest of the grass with 3051, 3347, and 471.

**STEP 1**

2. Fill the paws in with 3790, 3782, 822, and 3864. Use 224 for the toenails and 451 between the toes.

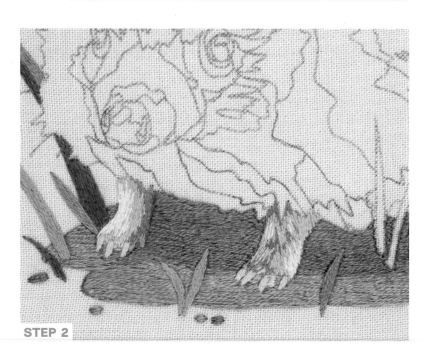

**STEP 2**

**3** Stitch the nose with 310, 3799, 04, 336, and 800. Fill in the eyes with 310, 800, 3799, 535, and White. Use 800 to add a highlight under the eye on the left and 04 for the highlight under the eye on the right.

STEP 3

**4** Fill the chest with 648, 07, 08, 3866, and 3782, paying close attention to the texture.

STEP 4

**5** Stitch the hedgehog's snout and cheeks with 08, 07, 451, 645, 3021, and 648. Fill in the center of the face, between the eyes, with 645, 648, and 3790.

STEP 5

**6** Stitch the ears with 3031, 3799, 535, 3862, and 310. Start at the bottom and work upward.

STEP 6

**7** Stitch the left side of the face with White, 3866, and 648. Fill in the forehead with White, 648, 07, and 3866. Finish the face with 648, 07, 451, 224, 822, and 3866 along the right side.

STEP 7

**8** Fill in the side and bottom of the body with 3782, 3033, and 3866. Avoid the blades of grass.

STEP 8

**9** Begin the quills along the main part of the back. See Stitching Spines (page 34) for additional guidance. Stitch them more loosely spaced near the rear of the hedgehog, refining them further as you move toward the forehead.

Start each group of spines by stitching a small area of shadow at the end of the spines on the right side with 646. Fill in the next section with 613. Use 3371, 611, 3782, 613, and 3865 to work in the quills. Leave space between where the fur and quills meet.

STEP 9

**10** Use the same colors from the previous step to stitch the quills on the forehead. Intermittently add a bit of highlight with 3799 and 645 over 3371 to add definition to the quills. Since these are closest to the face, they should appear most fully rendered.

STEP 10

**11** Add the hairs overlapping the quills with 648, 3790, and 3866, filling in the final gaps on the body.

STEP 11

**12** Stitch the remaining blades of grass in front of the hedgehog with 471, 3051, and 3347.

STEP 12

**13** Finish the portrait by stitching the whiskers with a split backstitch (see Portrait Accents, page 39) in dark gray-brown thread or Gütermann 2960.

STEP 13

# Horse | *Fatima*

**THIS HORSE PROJECT IS GOOD PRACTICE** for slightly changing the tone of a thread color. After stitching a base with one shade, you can slightly alter the tone by adding more vibrant top stitching—necessary for capturing the subtle shifts of light and color across the horse. This pattern was stitched on Kona Cotton in the color Natural. Use the Horse Pattern (page 140) to prepare the hoop.

Photo by Cintia Szuhai

Stitch direction guide

## THREAD COLORS

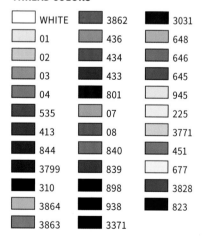

| | | |
|---|---|---|
| WHITE | 3862 | 3031 |
| 01 | 436 | 648 |
| 02 | 434 | 646 |
| 03 | 433 | 645 |
| 04 | 801 | 945 |
| 535 | 07 | 225 |
| 413 | 08 | 3771 |
| 844 | 840 | 451 |
| 3799 | 839 | 677 |
| 310 | 898 | 3828 |
| 3864 | 938 | 823 |
| 3863 | 3371 | |

*Did you know?*

*Horses cannot breathe through their mouths.*

Color guide

1  Reference the color guide, and begin with the body of the horse. Work from the upper back of the horse down to the bottom of the portrait. Use 310, 3371, 3031, 3799, 898, 801, and 3862 to create the shadows and highlights of the body. Fill in the darker areas of color first and then work to the lighter colors, top stitching to blend as needed.

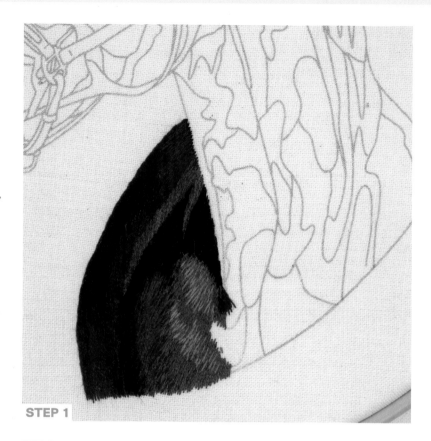

STEP 1

2  Fill the right side of the neck with 3031, 844, 08, 840, 04, and 535. Start at the bottom and work upward.

*tip* Sometimes brown horse fur can look gray in sunlight, as seen in this pattern.

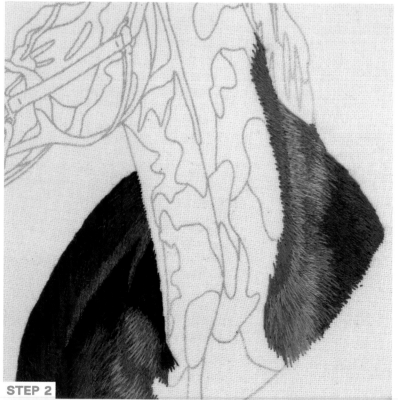

STEP 2

**3** Still working from the bottom of the portrait upward, fill in the middle of the lower neck with 3031, 801, 3863, 839, 3371, 938, 898, and 3862, completing the bottom edge of the portrait.

STEP 3

**4** Continue filling in the next section of the neck with 310, 3031, 898, 801, 08, 839, 844, 3862, 433, 02, and 535. Referencing the color guide, fill in the larger areas of color first before top stitching with small stitches of the other colors to blend.

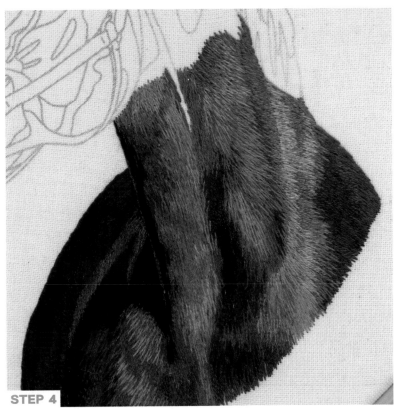

STEP 4

**5** Finish the upper neck with 3863, 535, 04, 08, 840, 801, 3862, 844, and 898. Blend each larger area of color with small top stitches so they do not look patchy.

Fill in the area of the jowl up to the halter with 844, 3371, and 898.

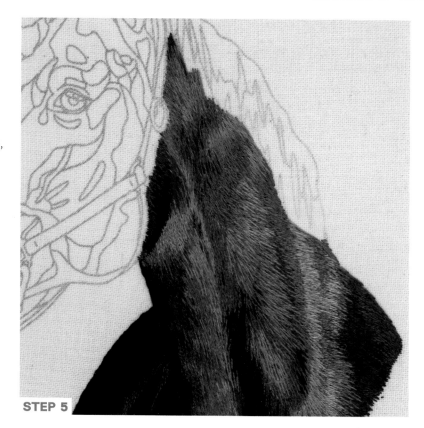

STEP 5

**6** Fill in the ears with 310. Add small inner ear hairs with 844, 3371, and 801. Stitch the brown fur on the back of the ears with 3862, 801, 3864, 3863, and 434.

STEP 6

**7** Create the eye by filling in the pupil and outlining the iris with 310. Use 938 to fill in the iris. Add a blue highlight above the pupil with 823. Highlight the eye with 04 and 02. Add an eyelid with 844, 535, 938, and 3864. Finally, use 310 to define the folds around the eyelids.

STEP 7

**8** Start filling in the left side of the face above the eye and then the forehead with 3371, 08, 310, and 3031. Add the white spot on the forehead with 01, 03, and White, paying close attention to stitch direction.

Continue moving to the right side of the face using 844, 801, 938, 433, 434, and 840. Add some lighter fur around the eye and temple with 3862, 3863, and 3864. Stitch some 3771 by the right ear. Use 535, 844, and 08 to create the gray highlights. Add a few top stitches of 03 to accent the gray highlights.

The horse's face will have a lot of subtle top stitching—remember that top stitching should follow the same direction as the threads it's stitched over

**9** Continue filling in the next portion of the face from right to left, until you reach the halter. Use 01 and 03 to make the white stripe down the snout. Use 3031, 535, 08, 07, 3863, and 3771 around the white stripe. Add some areas of shadow with 3862 and 433, and fill in the lighter middle of the face with 3863 and 3864. Top stitch with 3771 and 945. Fill in the right side of the face with 07, 3863, 433, 3864, 3862, 434, 436, 3031, and 844.

STEP 8

STEP 9

**10** Use 434, 844, 433, 3371, 898, and 3863 for the lower jowl below the halter. Add a shadow by the halter with 310.

STEP 10

**11** Add a harsh shadow with 3371 below the halter. Then, fill in the white of the snout with 02, White, and 03. Use 225 and 451 for the pink areas on the nose.

Working from the top of the snout down, use 3863, 3864, 3771, 945, 434, and 801 for the brown areas. Use 310, 646, 3799, and 413 for the nostril. Blend the gray and the brown near the lips with 648, 3864, 646, 844, and 645.

For the lower lip, use 310, 3799, 535, 3864, and 3863.

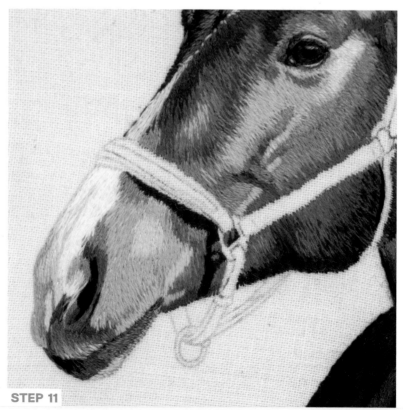

STEP 11

**12** Fill in the halter with 3799, 310, 535, and 04 for all the gray areas. Top stitch highlights along the edges of the halter with 03. Fill in the small area of fur near the jowl inside the circular ring with 3371. Finish the halter by using 677 and 3828 for the gold buckles and finishings.

STEP 12

**13** Finish the portrait by stitching the horse's mane with 310, 3799, 413, and 04. For the forehead hair, work from the top of the hair, near the ears, downward, building from dark to light colors. Down the neck, work from top to bottom, still moving from dark to light. Top stitch to blend as needed.

STEP 13

# Chicken | *Natasha*

**CHICKENS HAVE DIFFERENT TYPES OF FEATHERS ON THEIR BODIES—**some that can appear smooth, some that look like hair, and some that hold their feathery definition. Although the feathers are all stitched with the same colors, the angle and layering of the stitches will help each feather stand out. This pattern was stitched on Kona Cotton in the color Desert Green. Use the Chicken Pattern (page 140) to prepare the hoop.

Photo by Allison Funneman

Stitch direction guide

**THREAD COLORS**

| | | |
|---|---|---|
| WHITE | 400 | 839 |
| 310 | 975 | 224 |
| 3865 | 648 | 3712 |
| 738 | 646 | 3328 |
| 436 | 06 | 347 |
| 434 | 3860 | 3777 |
| 433 | 3033 | 3857 |
| 301 | 3782 | 3371 |
| 300 | 3790 | |
| 938 | 3862 | |

Color guide

*Did you know?*
*Not only do chickens recognize other chickens, but they can recognize human faces, too!*

1　Reference the color guide, and stitch the feathers near the bottom left of the portrait. Use 300, 975, 434, 436, 938, 839, 3862, and 738. See Feathers (page 33) for more information on stitching this texture.

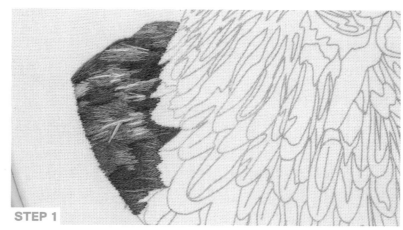

STEP 1

2　Work your way along the bottom of the portrait. Fill in the lower feathers, then move upward. Use angled backstitching to create the look of a feather and then add the shaft down the center. Make the white feather tufts with 648, 3865, and 738. Fill in the rest of the feathers with 300, 436, 975, 433, 3371, and 434.

STEP 2

3　Continue working until you reach the right side of the portrait, using 3371, 938, 300, 975, 433, and 434.

STEP 3

**4** Using the same colors, begin working up toward the chicken's neck. Stop under the wattle. Top stitch the less defined feathers that appear more like hair near the side of the neck.

STEP 4

**5** Working back toward the center of the portrait, fill in the next section of chest feathers with 3371, 938, 300, 975, 433, and 434. Make the feathers more vertically angled the closer you get to the head.

STEP 5

**6** Fill in the lower area of the back of the neck with 300, 3371, 938, 975, 433, and 434. Add a few highlights with 436. These feathers are smaller and more fur-like in appearance.

STEP 6

**7** Create the feathers on the back of the head with 300, 3371, 938, 975, 433, and 434. These feathers are smooth. Begin with the shadows, and top stitch in the lighter colors as needed.

STEP 7

**8** Stitch the eye by first filling in the pupil with 310. Use 3371 around the pupil. Work your way outward with 436, 301, and 400. Top stitch highlights with 646 and White. Outline the eye with 3371, and use 3860 for the tear-duct area.

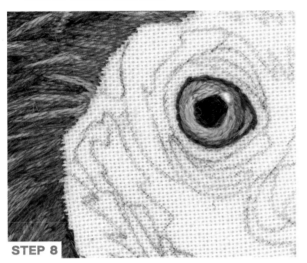

STEP 8

**9** For the beak, stitch with 3371, 06, 436, 3782, 3790, and 3033. Work from the top of the beak, at the nostril, down toward the point.

STEP 9

**10** Fill in the feathers on top of the head and below the beak with 300, 975, 938, and 3371. Use short, intermittent stitches as you move down the face.

STEP 10

**11** Create the wattles below and around the beak with small French knots (page 42) in 3777, 347, 3857, 3328, and 3712 stitched closely together. Add small French knot highlights with 224. Make the knots with one strand of thread and one wrap around the needle. Keep the knots close together for more solid-looking areas of color. Bring in a knot of a new color between two different color sections to blend them.

STEP 11

**12** Fill in the comb and the area above the nostrils using the same colors and stitches as Step 11. For the blended areas with several intermixed colors, stitch scattered French knots in the midtones, then add in the lighter tones, and finally add the darker colors. Stitch a small patch of feathers between the wattle and the comb, near the eye, with 300.

STEP 12

**13** Stitch the area around the eye using the same colors and stitches as Steps 11 and 12. Use small backstitches between the French knots to accent the rings of wrinkled skin. Add a few top stitches of 3857 into the feathers from Step 12.

STEP 13

**14** Using the same colors and stitches as Steps 11–13, stitch the chicken's earlobe—the round, oblong shape below the eye, at the bottom of the face.

STEP 14

**15** Finish the portrait by stitching the rest of the feathers with 938, 975, 300, 434, and 648. Use thread painting stitches instead of French knots. These feathers are smaller and look smoother and hairlike.

STEP 15

# Budgie | *Milo*

**THIS PORTRAIT WILL REQUIRE A LOT OF TINY STITCHES** once you reach the bird's head. Use a magnifying tool if you are finding it difficult to see where to place the stitches. This pattern was stitched on Kona Cotton in the color Natural. Use the Budgie Pattern (page 140) to prepare the hoop.

Photo by Mary Hilton

Stitch direction guide

## THREAD COLORS

| | | |
|---|---|---|
| WHITE | 841 | 519 |
| 01 | 840 | 597 |
| 02 | 3031 | 518 |
| 535 | 648 | 3810 |
| 3799 | 646 | 3808 |
| 310 | 645 | 158 |
| 3864 | 3021 | 733 |
| 3863 | 747 | 732 |
| 3862 | 162 | 730 |
| 3371 | 827 | 225 |
| 433 | 813 | 224 |
| 612 | 3840 | 3861 |
| 611 | 3807 | 632 |
| 3781 | 3761 | |
| 842 | 3766 | |

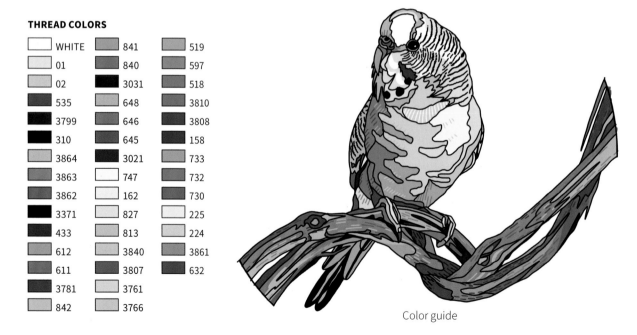

Color guide

## Did you know?

While most birds feet consist of three toes in the front and one in the back, Budgies and other parrot species have two toes in the front and two in the back.

1. Reference the color guide, and stitch the bird's tail into distinct feather sections with 310, 648, 646, 3799, 519, and 02. See Feathers (page 33) for more on stitching this texture. These feathers are long and skinny. Work from the longest feathers to the shorter ones at the top.

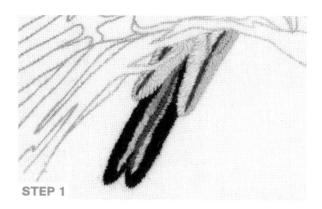

**STEP 1**

2. Fill in the swooping branches, working from the ones in the background to the ones in the foreground. Follow the stitch direction guide to create the bark-like texture of the branches. Remember that branches aren't perfectly smooth—they have chunks of texture and color, so don't blend the colors too much.

Use 3781, 3863, 3031, 611, 3862, 841, 840, 842, 3864, 612, and 433 for the branches. Create the cracks in the branches with 3371 and 3021. Work from the darker colors to the lighter ones, top stitching to blend sometimes.

*tip* **If you would like to use fewer colors, you can omit 611 and 612.**

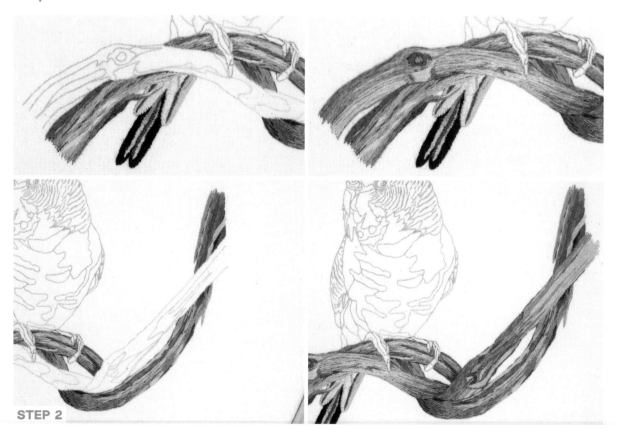

**STEP 2**

**3** Fill in the feet with small stitches of 224, 225, 632, and 3861.

STEP 3

**4** Fill in the lower portion of the left wing feathers with 3799, 645, 648, and 162. Finish the left wing by first stitching the stripes with 310, and then filling in between them with 648.

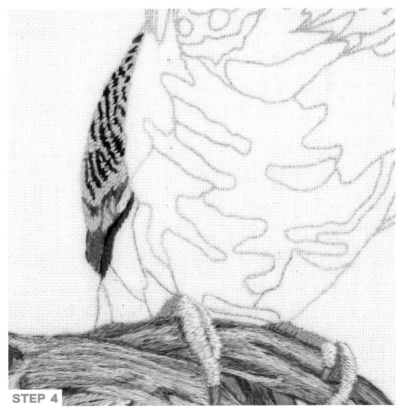

STEP 4

**5** Using the same stripe technique from Step 4, fill in the right wing with 813, 162, 645, 310, and 01.

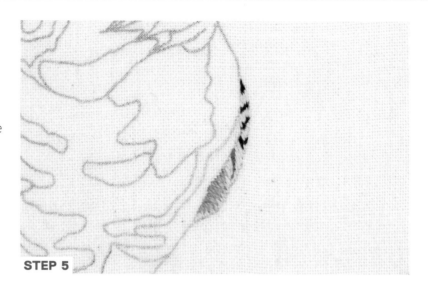

STEP 5

**6** Start filling in the bird's body from the bottom up. Use 645, 3808, 3810, 597, 827, and 518 near the bottom of the bird. Though these are feathers, they're smooth and soft, making the gradients more fur-like.

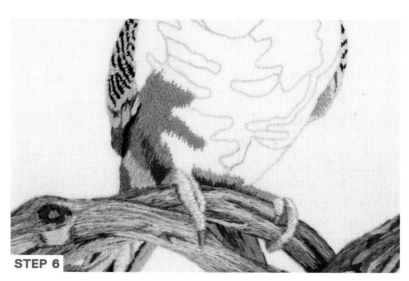

STEP 6

**7** Continue filling in the bird's chest, stitching up onto its shoulder with 519, 3761, 3766, and 827. Start with the midtones, and then add the shadows and highlights.

STEP 7

**8** Finish the bird's body with 827, 519, 3761, 3810, and 518. Add a large area of highlight with 747, and add a few additional bands of top stitching around the chest to highlight the feathers. Use 3766 to blend in the vibrant teal-blue feathers around the chest with top stitching.

STEP 8

**9** Stitch the beak with 733, 732, and 730. Add a shadow under the beak with 3799. Work from the top of the beak down to the tip. Create the nose above the beak with 597, 3807, 646, and 310.

Fill in the eye with 648, 310, White, and 3799.

**10** Fill in the forehead and the left edge of the head, below the beak, with 648, 646, 01, and White, closely following the stitch direction guide.

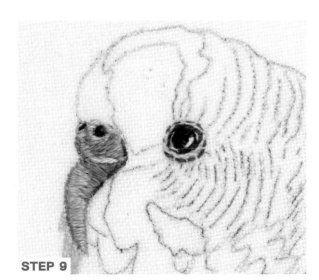

STEP 9

STEP 10

**11** Using the same stripe technique used on the wings (see Step 4), fill in the stripes down the side of the head with 310 and 535, then fill the remaining space with 01 and White. Top stitch over the stripes with 3799 to blend as needed.

STEP 11

**12** Stitch the striped area under the eye. First fill in the stripes with 535, and then fill in the remaining area between the stripes with 01 and White. Use 310 to add a few stitches of black feathers over 535.

STEP 12

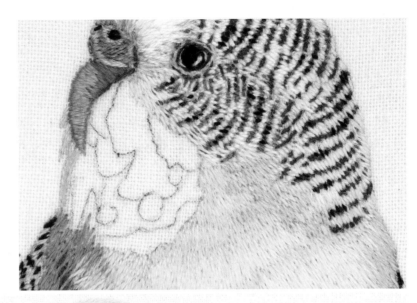

**13** Finish the portrait by using 3840, 3761, and 747 to stitch the remaining blue areas of feathers. Then use 310, 645, 648, 01, White, to fill in the final gaps and add a patch of dark blue feathers with 158.

STEP 13

# Snake | *Viggo*

**USE A STACKED BRICK STITCH** (see Scales, page 35) to create the scales and work row by row in small sections. Make sure to follow the stitch direction guide with the brick stitch to capture the way a snake's body bends. Further accent the curvature by adding shadows and highlights. This pattern was stitched on Kona Cotton in the color Natural. Use the Snake Pattern (page 140) to prepare the hoop.

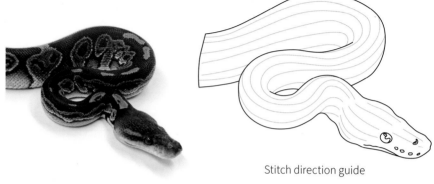

Photo by Kendall Thornhill

Stitch direction guide

### THREAD COLORS

| | |
|---|---|
| WHITE | 3790 |
| 04 | 3031 |
| 413 | 08 |
| 3799 | 613 |
| 310 | 612 |
| 3033 | 3863 |
| 3782 | 3859 |

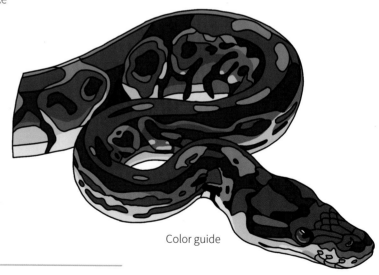

Color guide

## Note

*For the whole snake project, use a stacked brick stitch (see Scales, page 35), stitched with 2 strands of thread, unless otherwise noted. You may find it helpful to have multiple needles threaded at once, switching out the colors and needles as you go. The snake has many distinct color sections, so there isn't the need for much blending or gradients. The snake is stitched progressively from back to front until you reach the head.*

*Did you know?*
Adult ball pythons typically shed every four to six weeks.

**1** Use the same colors throughout the snake's body: 3033, 3031, 3799, 3782, 3790, 08, 3863, 413, and 04.

Reference the color guide, and begin stitching at the left end of the snake. The brick stitches should become smaller as you move toward the snake's neck. Follow the stitch direction guide to pay close attention to how to angle the rows of brick stitch to create the curve of the snake's body.

*tip* **You will see areas of shadow and highlight on the color guide that will not be shown in the instructional photos as you stitch along the snake. This is top stitching and will be done in Step 11. If you prefer, you may add the shadow and highlight top stitching as you go.**

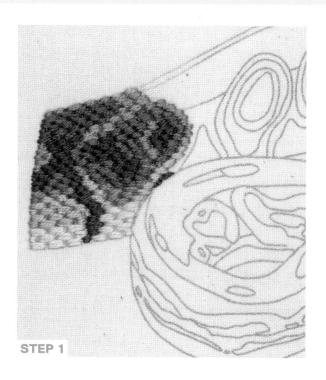

STEP 1

**2** Move to the middle back of the snake and stitch with 3799, 3031, 08, 3782, and 3790. The brick stitches should start to slightly angle upward in this area.

**3** Keep working into the first inner curve of the snake with 3782, 3033, 3790, 08, 3863, 413, and 3799. Start to curve the brick stitch down slightly.

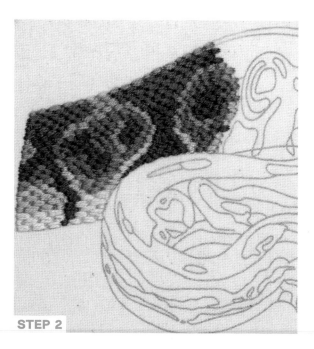

STEP 2

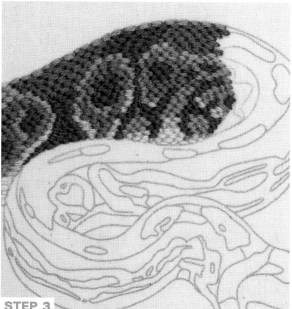

STEP 3

**4** Create the bend of the snake's body, working around the curve along the top edge of the snake. Use 3782, 3790, 08, 3863, 413, and 3799. Add new rows of scales as you come around the outer edge. Drop rows of brick stitch as needed when they start to blend into each other.

**5** Using the same colors as the previous step, fill in the next portion of the snake's body, up until the next curve.

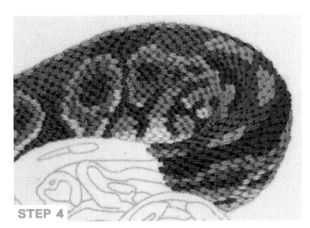

STEP 4

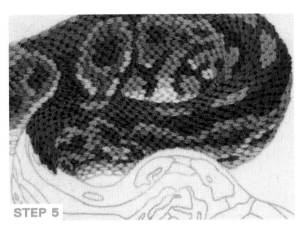

STEP 5

**6** Continue working through the next curve with 3033, 3782, 3790, 08, 3863, 413, and 3799, repeating the process from Step 4, adding and dropping rows as needed.

**7** Fill in the neck of the snake with 3033, 3782, 3790, 08, 3863, 413, 310, and 3799. Curve the brick stitch upward and then back down again to follow the contour lines of the snake's body in the stitch direction guide.

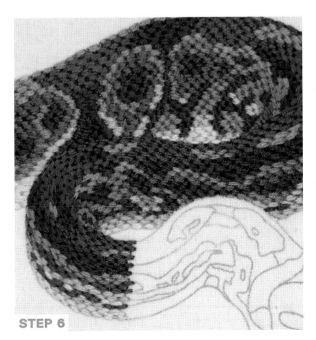

STEP 6

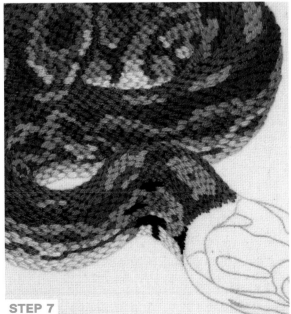

STEP 7

**8** Create the eye with 310, 413, 04, and White using long and short stitch, top stitching, and 1 strand of thread.

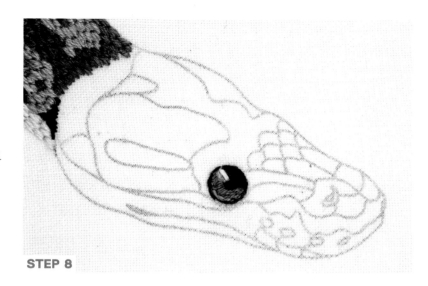

STEP 8

**9** Using 1 strand of thread and long and short stitch, begin creating scales near the snake's jaw with 3033, 3790, 3782, 613, 612, 3799, 413, and 08. Use 3859 to create the snake's scent holes along the upper lip. Stitch from the nose up to the eye with 3799 and 04. While using 1 strand of thread, keep the appearance of scales by making backstitches in distinct sections.

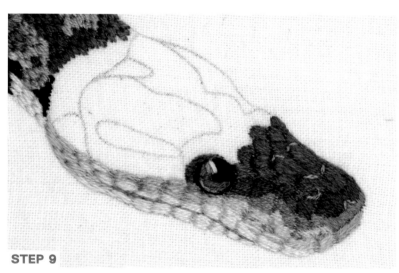

STEP 9

**10** Fill in the remainder of the head by using brick stitches with 3799, 413, 3790, 08, and 3782. The brick stitches for the scales should be larger by the front of the head and smaller near the back of the head.

STEP 10

**11** Finish the portrait by top stitching some shadows and highlights along the snake's scales. Using 2 strands of thread, first add highlights with 04 over stitches of 413. Next, use 310 over stitches of 3799 to add shadow along the bottom of the snake. This will give the snake's body more form and dimensionality.

**STEP 11**

# Betta Fish | *Dalí*

**THE BETTA FISH'S BEAUTIFUL TAIL CAN BE OVERWHELMING TO STITCH.** Take it one section at a time, and work row by row unless there's a large section of one color. Follow the curved lines of the betta's tail to capture the delicate way it floats through the water. This pattern was stitched on Kona Cotton in the color Fog. Use the Betta Fish Pattern (page 140) to prepare the hoop.

Photo by Ellie's Exotics

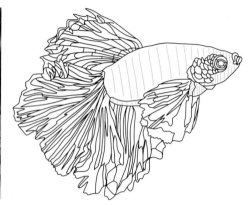

Stitch direction guide

**THREAD COLORS**

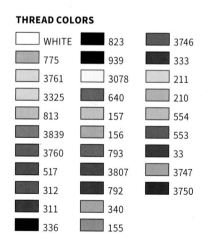

| | | |
|---|---|---|
| WHITE | 823 | 3746 |
| 775 | 939 | 333 |
| 3761 | 3078 | 211 |
| 3325 | 640 | 210 |
| 813 | 157 | 554 |
| 3839 | 156 | 553 |
| 3760 | 793 | 33 |
| 517 | 3807 | 3747 |
| 312 | 792 | 3750 |
| 311 | 340 | |
| 336 | 155 | |

Color guide

## *Did you know?*

*Although this betta fish looks purple, most betta fish actually have complex layers of iridescent and varied color scales that only appear purple.*

**1** For the fish's scales, use a vertical stacked brick stitch (see Scales, page 35) and 2 strands of thread. Reference the color guide, then begin stitching the fish's scales near the base of the tail fin. Work across the fish to the top of the head. Start with small brick stitches, and gradually increase the size of the stitch as you work toward the middle of the fish. Use 155, 156, 333, 3746, 340, 793, and 157 for the scales. As you move onto the fish's head, switch to long and short stitch, but keep the appearance of scales by stitching in distinct vertical sections.

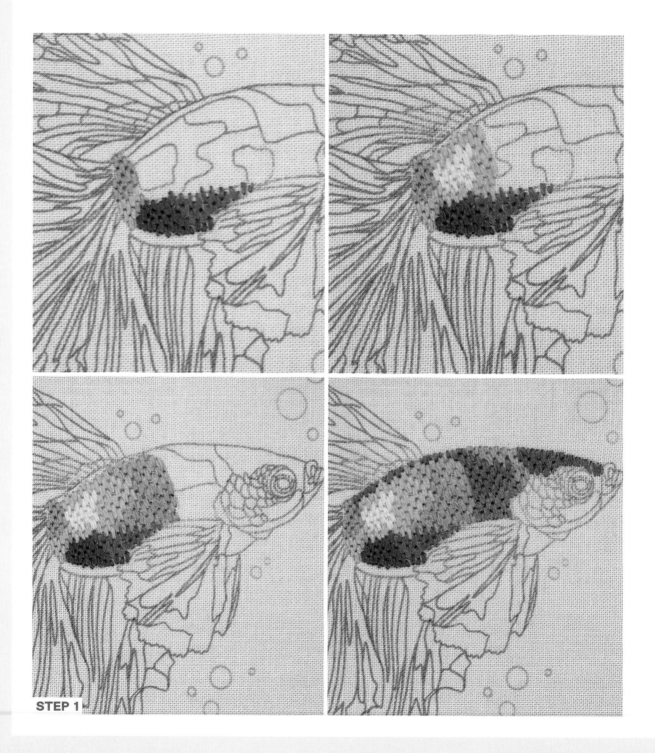

STEP 1

**2** Use 1 strand of thread to stitch the eye and mouth. Use 333, 155, 3746, 311, and 939 to stitch the eye. Add highlights in the eye with 640 and 3760. Use 340 for the eyelid. For the mouth, use 333, 155, and 156. Add shadows and highlights with 939 and 157.

STEP 2

**3** Use 2 strands of thread in 3746, 3807, 793, 155, and 823 to fill in the rest of the face. Fill in the remaining small area of the fish's belly below the gills with 2 strands of 155. Don't use brick stitch for this section, but refer to the color guide and fill in each section separately to keep up the appearance of scales.

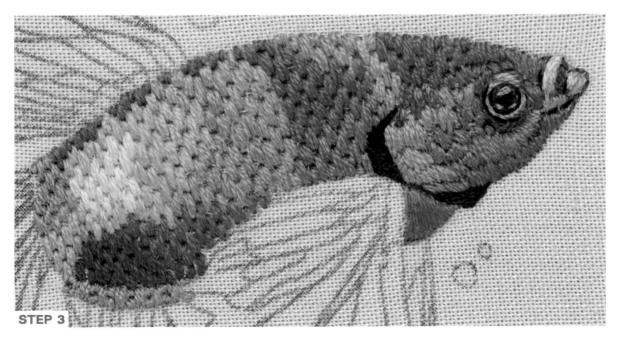

STEP 3

**4** Using 1 strand of thread, define the scales by stitching between them, adding 1 stitch to the left of each brick stitch. Use 792 around 155. Use 3807 around 157 and 156. Use 792 around 340. Use 336 around 3746, 333, and 3807. Use 792 around 793.

Slightly blend the scales by stitching 1 or two small straight stitches into neighboring color areas on top of the brick stitches. Blend 340 into 3746, 157 into 156, and 155 into 793.

STEP 4

**5** Moving on to the fins and tail, continue using 1 strand of thread and long and short stitch. Begin by filling in the small visible piece of the back pectoral fin with 333, 340, 3807, and 336.

STEP 5

**6** Stitch the pectoral fin in the foreground. Begin by filling in the blocks of color. Then, go back and define the fin rays with shadows and highlights. For the darker purple areas, use 333, 3746, 775, and 155. For the blue–purple areas, use 157, 156, and 793. For the pink accents, use 553, 554, and 211.

STEP 6

**7** Define the fin by adding brighter highlights and shadows with 792, 3746, 157, 336, and 3761.

STEP 7

**8** Stitch the fin rays (the fanlike lines down the fins) on the anal fin with 336. Use 3747, 333, and 155 to stitch the upper middle area of the fin between the rays.

For the pink areas, use 33 and 553. For the lighter colors and the blue tones near the bottom of the fin, use 775, 3325, 157, 155, and 3839. Use 336 and 3807 to add some dark shadows near the bottom of the fin.

**STEP 8**

**9** Define the anal fin by top stitching with 792 and 336, creating more rays. Add highlights with 340.

**STEP 9**

**10** On the lower half of the tail fin, stitch the highlights with 157, 3325, 813, and 156. Then, fill in between them with 333, 33, 3746, 340, 517, 3760, 553, and 311.

**STEP 10**

**11** For the upper tail fin, work section by section, starting at the base of the tail fin and moving out to the edge. Use 3839, 157, 336, 156, 3325, 813, 312, and 3760 for the areas of blue. Use 33 and 553 for the pink areas. Use 333, 340, and 3746 for the areas of purple.

Stitch the small folded area of the tail fin with 33, 3746, 340, 3839, 156, 312, and 553. Add highlights with 775 and 3325.

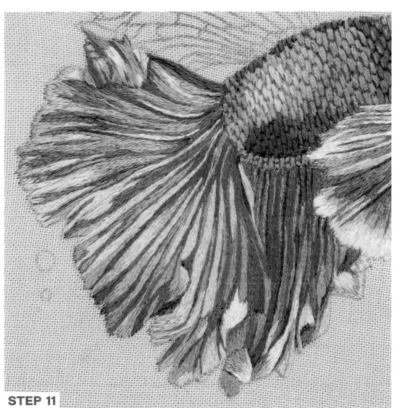

**STEP 11**

**12** Finish the tail fin by adding definition with 312, 336, 157, 210, 340, 156, and 3839. Add highlights with 775 and 157.

STEP 12

**13** Stitch the dorsal fin rays with 3746. Fill between them, working from the base of the fin out to the upper tips. Use 155 near the body, and as you move up, use 312, 157, 3839, 156, and 340, and then 333, 3746, 210, 156, and 3807. Use 33 and 553 for the pink areas.

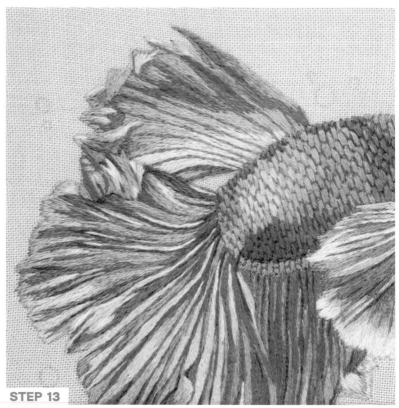

STEP 13

**STEP 14**

**14** Define the dorsal fin with 336, 312, 3750, and 792.

**15** Finish the portrait by adding bubbles around the fish with 3078, 340, 3325, and White. Use 1 strand of thread and split backstitches (see Portrait Accents, page 39). Use French knots (page 42) with 2 strands of thread for additional small bubbles.

**STEP 15**

# Bearded Dragon | *Sushi*

**FOR THIS PORTRAIT, I CHOSE TO REST THE BEARDED DRAGON ON A BRANCH** instead of on a hand, as pictured. This creates more of a natural scene and an interesting composition. I used a separate reference for the branch. You may want to use multiple threaded needles at once for the scales. This

Photo by Emily Streich

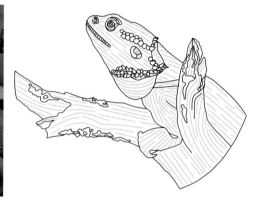

Stitch direction guide

pattern was stitched on Kona Cotton in the color Natural. Use the Bearded Dragon Pattern (page 140) to prepare the hoop.

**THREAD COLORS**

| | | |
|---|---|---|
| 3033 | 646 | 434 |
| 3032 | 645 | 3047 |
| 3790 | 02 | 3046 |
| 05 | 413 | 3064 |
| 06 | 310 | 3864 |
| 07 | 712 | 3863 |
| 08 | 3821 | 3862 |
| 841 | 729 | 945 |
| 840 | 976 | 3771 |
| 839 | 301 | 3012 |
| 3031 | 300 | 3011 |
| 3371 | 436 | |
| 648 | 435 | |

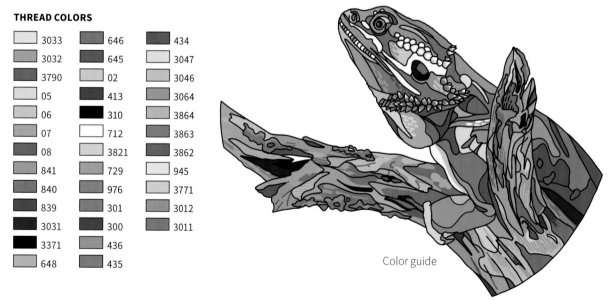

Color guide

*Did you know?*

*Lightning bugs, or fireflies, are toxic to bearded dragons.*

**1** Reference the color guide, then begin the portrait with the lower branch. Use 839, 07, 841, 840, 645, 06, 648, and 05 to fill in the wood grains. Work from the darker cracks in the branch to the lighter highlights or section by section.

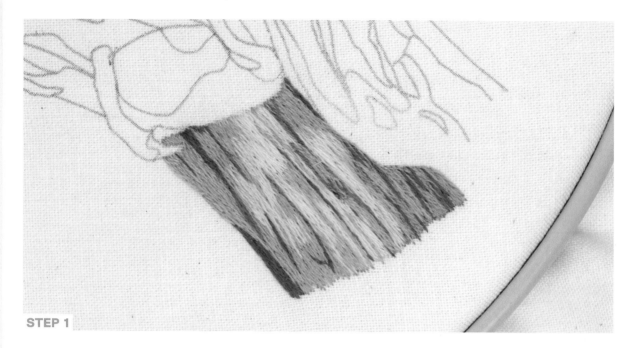

STEP 1

**2** Skipping the vertical branch for now, move to the middle portion of the lower branch. Work from the lizard's hand toward the left. Use 07, 645, 839, 646, 841, 648, 06, 840, and 08. Add some lighter areas to the branch with 3033. Use 3371 and 3031 for the darker cracks in the branch.

STEP 2

**3** Fill in the remaining area of the horizontal branch with 3371, 3031, 06, 07, 839, 646, 645, 3790, and 3032. This portrait should extend to the edges of the hoop when displayed, so add a little extra stitching to each end of the branch to avoid leaving any gaps between the embroidery and the hoop.

STEP 3

**4** Accent the branch by adding some moss. Use French knots (page 42) and colors 3011 and 3012. Optionally, you can save this step until the end of the portrait, after the completion of the vertical branch, and stitch all the moss at the same time.

STEP 4

**5** Fill in the lizard's back with a stacked brick stitch (see Scales, page 35). Use 2 strands of thread with colors 976, 434, 729, 301, 3790, 08, and 300. To blend the colors, top stitch over the brick stitches.

> *Note* ————————
>
> **Blending The Lizard's Scales**
> *Blend the areas of color with top stitching as you go, or wait until you finish an area and then go back and add top stitching to the section as a whole.*

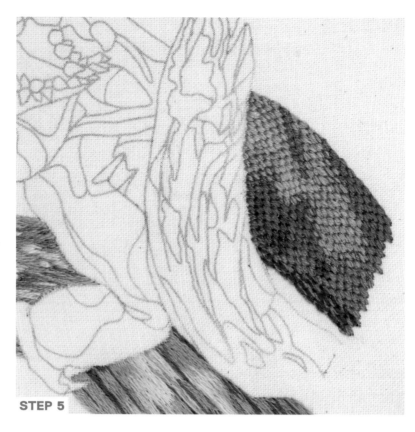

**STEP 5**

**6** Beginning near the armpit, fill in the shoulder and upper arm. Make the brick stitches curve around the armpit and continue down the arm toward the wrist. Use 3033, 945, 3863, 976, 3821, and 712, and accent the shadow in the armpit with 300 and 08.

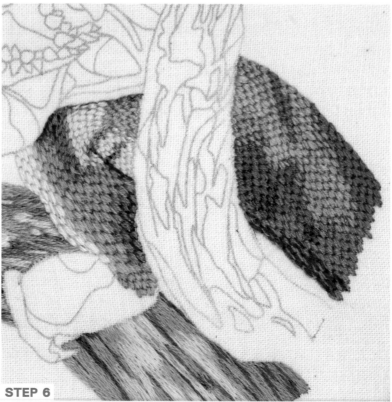

**STEP 6**

**7** Use brick stitches of 436, 3046, 729, and 3047 to fill in the foot and wrist. Add claws with long and short stitches of 3064 and 3771. Add a crease in the inner elbow with 300.

STEP 7

**8** Resume using brick stitch to fill in the area behind the lizard's head with 976, 729, 3821, 08, 3864, 646, 712, 645, and 945.

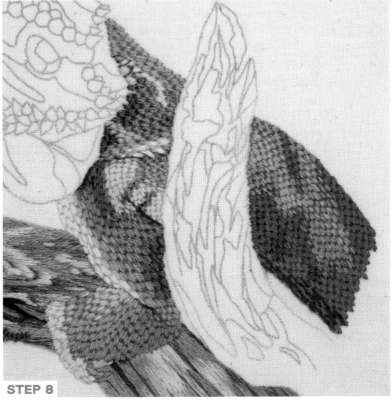

STEP 8

**9** Stitch the lower area of the neck and jowl with 3790, 648, 646, 645, 3033, 301, and 976. Pay attention to the angle and curve of the scales in the stitch direction guide.

STEP 9

**10** Fill in the chin and lower area of the face with 3046, 300, 729, 3863, and 976. Then thread paint the lizard's beard spikes with 1 strand of thread and colors 729, 976, 712, and 08. Work from the base of each spine to the tip, stitching from the darkest colors in the background to the lighter colors in the foreground. Add a shadow with 08 between the spikes for definition.

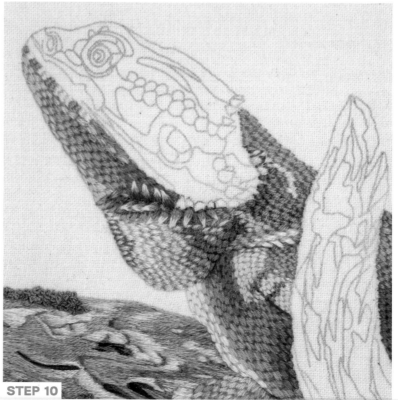

STEP 10

**11** Use 1 strand of 310, 413, 02, and 07 to thread paint the eye. Make the eyelid by using 3031, 729, 976, 3047, 300, and 08. Fill in the nostril with 1 strand of 3862.

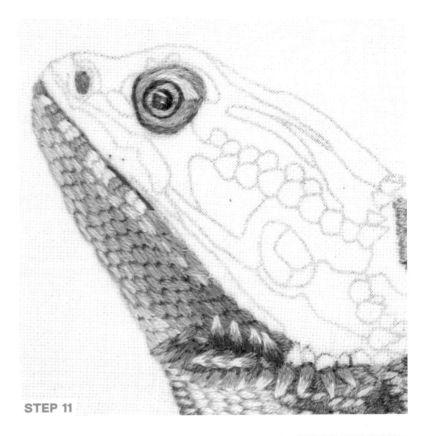

**STEP 11**

**12** Starting with the area near the nose, work your way down the middle area of the face to join the neck. Use 2 strands of 729, 841, 712, 976, 435, 3046, 3790, 301, 3821, 300, and 08 and resume the stacked brick stitch. Use 1 strand of thread when creating the rest of the lizard's spikes. Fill in the earhole with 3031, 3371, and 646.

**STEP 12**

**13** Stitch the top of the head with 2 strands of thread and brick stitch. Use 435, 729, 712, 301, 3821, 3046, 436, and 3031. Switch back to thread painting with 1 strand of thread to add the rest of the spines on the head, using the same technique from Step 10.

STEP 13

**14** Move to the vertical branch. Using 1 strand of thread and long and short stitch, fill in the lower section of the branch with 840, 3031, 645, 646, 839, 07, 06, 648, 3033, 08, 841, and 3371. Work from the bottom of the branch up to the top. Start with darker colors, then continue to the lighter colors, top stitching as needed.

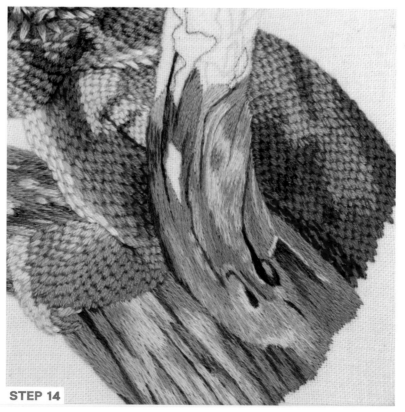

STEP 14

**15** Use 08, 07, 645, 3371, 648, 06, 3033, and 3031 for the remaining top portion of the branch.

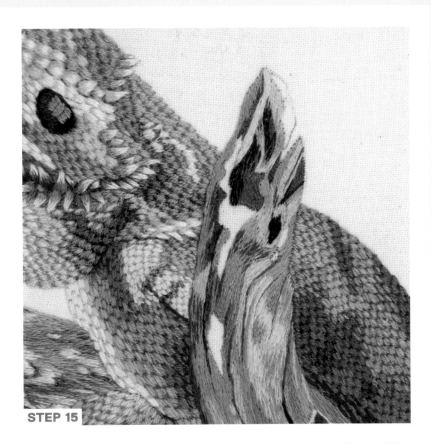

STEP 15

**16** Add French knot moss to the branch with 3011 and 3012.

STEP 16

# PATTERNS

   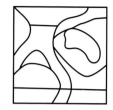

Texture Pattern Practice

Scan this QR code or visit tinyurl.com/11572-patterns-download
to access a downloadable PDF.

Rabbit

Guinea Pig

Hamster

**Enlarge 200%.**

Rat

Hedgehog

Ferret

Snake

Horse

Chicken

**Enlarge 200%.**

Budgie

Betta Fish

Flower Accent

Bearded Dragon

Wreath Accent

Aa Bb Cc Dd Ee Ff
Gg Hh Ii Jj Kk
Ll Mm Nn Oo Pp Qq
Rr Ss Tt Uu Vv Ww
Xx Yy Zz
1 2 3 4 5 6 7 8 9 0 ! ? &

Cursive Letter Accent Pattern

# Aa Bb Cc Dd Ee Ff
# Gg Hh Ii Jj Kk Ll
# Mm Nn Oo Pp Qq
# Rr Ss Tt Uu Vv Ww
# Xx Yy Zz
# 1 2 3 4 5 6 7 8 9 0 ! ? &

Script Letter Accent Pattern

# RESOURCES

Here are some useful links that will help you on your own embroidery journey.

## SUPPLIES

### Thread

**DMC**

dmc.com

**Gütermann**

123stitch.com

### Fabric and Stabilizer

**Kona Cotton from Robert Kaufman Fabrics**

robertkaufman.com/fabrics/kona_cotton/

**Sulky Fabri-Solvy Stabilizer**

sulky.com

### Needles

**Bohin needles**

boutique.bohin.com

### Embroidery Hoops

**Frank A. Edmunds embroidery hoops**

faedmunds.com/embroidery-hoops/

## ADDITIONAL RESOURCES

**Thread color conversion chart:**

cyberstitchers.com/stitching_tools/floss_conversion_charts

# ABOUT THE AUTHOR

Michelle Staub is a self-taught embroidery artist who has been bringing pet portraits to life through needle and thread since 2014. After years honing her skills, she now teaches others how to embroider their own pet portraits as well.

Ohio raised, she creates unique keepsakes for animal lovers around the world. Despite the chaos of chasing around her son, dog, and three cats, she still finds time for embroidery.

Her pet portraits have been featured in magazines, on television, and on websites around the world. You can find her work on her website and Instagram.

Use the tag #EmbroideredAnimalPortrait to share embroidery made with this book or your very own pet portraits!

*Visit Michelle online and follow on social media!*

**Website:** stitchingsabbatical.com

**Facebook:** /stitchingsabbatical

**Instagram:** @stitchingsabbatical

**YouTube:** /stitchingsabbatical